Fl Bass Fishing

Locations and Techniques for Largemouth and Peacock Bass Fishing in Florida

Chris Lutz

Copyright © 2018 Lutz

All rights reserved.

ISBN:9781718112131

DEDICATION

I dedicate this book to my Dad for introducing me to fishing in Florida.

Contents

Florida, A Bass Fishing Paradise	10
A Multi-Million Dollar Recreational Pastime	13
Guides: The Best Fishing Experience in Florida	15
An Adventure for the Whole Family	21
Bass Fishing in Central Florida	24
The St. Johns River	32
Lake Okeechobee and The Everglades	34
Urban Bass Fishing	39
Peacock Bass Fishing	41
Finding the Fish	46
Must Have Tackle for Florida Waters	50
Lure Types and Techniques	75
Catch and Release Practices	107
Fishing Ethics and Etiquette	109
How to Plan and Budget Your Florida Fishing Trip	113
Florida Bass Fishing Top Spots	127
About The Author	133

ACKNOWLEDGMENTS

I'd like to acknowledge all of my angler friends in Florida who have helped me gain the knowledge of fishing in Florida.

Florida, A Bass Fishing Paradise

For many people, the best bass fishing is to be found in Florida. Everyone wants to go there, and once you have fished for bass in Florida, you will certainly want to return again.

What's So Great About Florida?

The state's warm climate encourages fish to grow very large, and in many places there is so little fishing pressure that the bass are eager to bite at whatever is before them.

There's no doubt that there's great fishing in Florida. In fact, many lures that were unsuccessful in other parts of the country may work when you use them in Florida. And you don't always need to be on a boat in order to go fishing. In many parts of the country, you can't get to the fish unless you have a boat to get out on the water. But, with so many bodies of water in Florida, and many smaller ones at that, you can often find ample opportunities to catch fish right from shore. Or you can walk between a group of bodies of water attacking each one individually.

For anyone who identifies themselves as an angler, Florida is the place to be. Fishing is a dominant aspect of life in nearly the entire state. It's the sunshine state. There likely won't be many days that go by without a healthy dose of sunshine allowing you a good day of fishing. I'm a Florida native from Jacksonville. It's my home state and I love every inch of it.

Only Mexico and California rival Florida in the quality of bass fishing to be found. For many people who love fishing, there is no better place to call home than Florida. For some people, Florida bass fishing becomes such an addiction that they will change their lives for the ability to have greater opportunity to fish for bass in Florida more often. Some fishing enthusiasts have even been known to uproot their entire families, life, home, career and all, just to have the chance to live in Florida. I did. That's how amazing Florida bass fishing can be. Whether you reach that level of devotion or not, Florida bass fishing is an experience that everyone should try at least once.

The Downside of Florida Bass Fishing

It is important to remember weather concerns when looking at Florida bass fishing. Although it is the sunshine state, hurricane season is a risky time for all, and many storms have caused great devastation in different areas of Florida. In fact, moving to Florida for the fishing is something that is done with a great potential for pleasure and good fishing, but can also incur incredible risks for you and everything you own. Whether living there or just visiting, it is crucial that you think about the possible effects of a huge storm.

Even the regular summer thunderstorms, which can materialize and come up very quickly can be deadly. Florida is the lightning capital and it kills. The state of Florida has more thunderstorms than anywhere else in the United States. Especially if you are out on open water when it approaches. Boats are the highest things on the water after all, and a bass boat with metal all over it and fishing rods that can attract lightning is particularly dangerous. A person on such a boat when this happens is at serious risk or injury or perhaps even death. Summer storms are usually late afternoons, but can occur any time. Early morning fishing expeditions are probably safer during this time. Be sure to make your bass fishing decisions taking all factors into consideration.

Southwest Florida has gained worldwide acknowledgment for its incomparable saltwater fishing, but the outstanding freshwater fishing has not yet captured the wide spread concentration of its visitors. Local residents are in on the secret. This is shown on the three extremely "full of life" freshwater clubs in Collier County.

It will go down in history as the "Year of the Hurricanes." The constant pounding Florida took during the late summer of 2005 ranks as one of the largest natural disasters to ever strike the sunshine state. It was chaos at the time, but six months later, there were some positive things happening.

Although the enormous influx of rainwater unfavorably impacted both freshwater and saltwater fishing for several months, it did some good things for the inland lakes. Many were at low levels and the added needed freshwater was. In some respects, the hurricanes are a key part of a natural drawdown-refill cycle that will pay dividends for bass fishermen in future years.

A Multi-Million Dollar Recreational Pastime

Bass fishing represents one of the most popular fishing types practiced today. Its popularity has yielded a multi-billion dollar industry unto itself, aside from the business of other modes of sport fishing. In addition to rods and tackle, there are boats on the market designed specifically for bass fishing. Clothes and other gear are also very popular. Those are the larger ticket items you would expect to drive the recreational economy.

Freshwater sport fishing in Florida provided recreational opportunities for over 1.32 million people over age 16 and generated an economic output of $2.4 billion in 2006. Aside from that, Florida freshwater recreational fishing generated 19,519 jobs with earnings of $484 million in 2001. Florida freshwater fishing provided 20.8 million angler days of recreation (92% resident) based on 14.5 million trips. A trip is from the time someone leaves home until they return and may include many days.

Fishing might as well be baseball in Florida. The state agencies care very much about how it affects the economy overall and the tourist experience. In many places, fishing is seen as a nuisance or something you're not allowed to do very often. Just look at how many no fishing signs are posted at bodies of water in other states. Florida expects and wants you to fish the waterways.

I have personally been approached by FWC representatives for survey information. To get an idea of how specific and how detailed the information is they wish to gather, imagine one of the questions asked being how much we spent on snacks for our day of fishing. They wanted to know right down to the cent. Even though that was a question about food, it was the act of going fishing that caused us to put that money into the economy and the state cares about that. Without a doubt, Florida does more to encourage and protect fishing opportunities than any other state in my opinion.

Guides: The Best Fishing Experience in Florida

Even a seasoned bass fisherman may need guidance from bass fishing guides when out of his or her own backyard. No matter how skilled you may be, it is in your best interest to work with a guide when you initially begin bass fishing in a new place. Bass fishing guides don't just teach people how to fish. They can also help clients locate the best spots to score a great catch.

The main key for you is to find the most skilled and professional guides to educate you first about the industry and raise the right questions about it. Or else you will just be puzzled with the precise thing to do or get lost in a maze or a plethora of locations to go.

Clients are searching for the most dependable and credible guide that they can run into for them to get the best service they want. There are many bass fishing guide resources that you can rely on. Most of them could be found on the internet through their websites. Many are lodging locations that have guiding services on site.

Some of Florida's well-known and credible bass fishing locations, whether in terms of its quality and quantity, are almost guaranteed for bass fishing success, although nothing is ever a 100% certainty. Much of the fun is in the process of learning. Guides offer a lot of discount fishing packages you can avail. Some implement the no bass, no pay policy. True credible bass fishing guides will be able to help you find which spots to go to and what conditions are the best. Primarily, they can boost your chances of landing the big one on your Florida bass fishing trip.

Top water fishing is particularly great early in the morning and just before dark. It can be thrilling to watch the fish aggressively strike at your lures with all of their might.

Florida has a wealth of fishing environments and ecosystems to tackle, from small ponds to the swamps to interior streams and lakes. Florida chartered fishing trips and vacations can be planned for individuals, groups or families, and it all depends on what you want to do. Many fishermen heading south to Florida waters want to try both fresh and saltwater fishing, so charter companies in Florida are readily available both online and off to answer questions and provide schedules and pricing guidelines. Certain species may crossover or live in brackish waters together which may offer up the opportunity to catch bass and then maybe a redfish back to back which is an interesting experience.

If you want to split your fishing into both fresh and salt environments, narrow your search to find chartering opportunities that offer both. Many offer a wide variety of services, at reasonable costs, either on the internet or through your local travel agency. Better yet, find where you want to fish and then call down to local Chamber of Commerce offices in those areas for a listing of local charter services. Then, always follow up with a call or logon to the BBB's database to make sure the company you want to deal with is on the up and up.

When planning to do a charter on vacation, determine ahead of time how many people are going to be in your party, what it is you want to fish for, and how many days you're wanting. Doing so will help your potential charter business determine a more specific cost for you. Many Florida charter companies offer a wealth of fishing opportunities, whether you want to fly fish, or shore fly fish, wade fishing, or drift fishing. They may offer you opportunities to not only fish from the deck, but to anchor in coves or inlets and take you ashore. That's why it's best to come up with your own special wish list, and then go from there when speaking to any charter company representative for options and prices.

Always ask beforehand what services they offer, including food, lodging, as well as half day, full day, or longer chartered opportunities. If possible, check to make sure the boat and captain and crew you're chartered are legally licensed and that the boat is in good working order, complete with adequate numbers of life vests, and other safety equipment in case of rough weather or accidents. While many experienced adults, anglers or not, scoff at such topics, weather in Florida often changes quickly, and it's better to be prepared.

Planning a chartered fishing vacation in Florida should be fun, and not filled with hassles and problems. You can judge future service on board by service provided when you make that call, so pay attention to attitude, willingness to help as well as pricing. If you feel uncertain, try making additional calls until you find exactly what you're looking for. Chartering a vessel isn't cheap, so make sure that you take your time to get your money's worth.

Florida has the best big bass and extremely knowledgeable guides and they can furnish references to back it up. They are very well-mannered, experienced professional guides that will take you to these fish. They don't do the actual fishing for you, but they will show you the best places to go as well as show you some of their techniques. You get to set the hook and experience the fight of the fish yourself. Florida bass fishing guides fish the lakes on a daily basis, just to ensure your success.

Look for guides at these Florida locations:

-Lake Okeechobee
-Farm 13/Stick Marsh

-Lake Kissimmee
-Lake Toho
-Harris chain of lakes

Of course, there are literally thousands of terrific fishing spots in Florida but here are some of the top fishing spots:

-LAKE HARRIS. A 13,000 acre lake near Leesburg, FL. You can access it from Singletary Park.

-LAKE JACKSON. Located just north of Tallahassee, this shallow 4,000-acre natural lake is best around the Church Cove and Cattle Gap areas in the north and central portions.

-LAKE TARPON is located in Pinellas County on Florida's west coast about 25 miles northwest of Tampa. Suggested areas for the best fishing are: edges of cattails and bulrush, offshore clumps of vegetation, and near Brooker creek at the canal on the south end of the lake.

-TENOROC AREA. Formerly a phosphate mine less than 10 miles northeast of Lakeland, this 6,400-acre property is a series of marshes and small lakes.

-THE EVERGLADES. The two best areas are 210 square miles of Everglades marsh connected with perimeter canals, and 730 square miles of wetlands bordered by a canal system.

-STICK MARSH RESERVOIR. Created by the flooding of some 6,500 acres of former farmland, this is an abundant place for bass - the southern portion of Farm 13 is best.

-LAKE OKEECHOBEE. Probably Florida's most famous bass fishing location, Lake Okeechobee (the "Big O") is located in south central Florida, covering 730 square miles and is easily accessible from both the east and west coast of Florida. The best spots are around Eagle Bay Island, Fish eating Bay, and Pelican Bay.

-LAKE WOEHKAYAPKA, meaning "Walk-in-Water," is a 7,534-acre lake off S.R. 60 about 50 miles south of Orlando, a few miles east of Lake Wales, and very near to Lake Kissimmee.

-LAKE KISSIMMEE. Actually part of a chain of lakes in Polk and Osceola counties, Lake Kissimmee is 35,000 acres. Also known for great fishing is West Lake Tohopekaliga, an 18,810-acre shallow lake just south of the city of Kissimmee. It can be accessed by passing through the locks between the lakes. Another bass fishing guide in Florida is the so-called "Freelancer," which has been in business since 1970 and is considered as the oldest continuously operated guide service even before the arrival of others. All Freelancer guides have years of experience guiding on the Kissimmee Chain of Lakes. They know the latest techniques for catching big bass in Florida's grassy waters, which they claim as their edge over other bass fishing guide. Important features of the Freelancer are reasonable rates for 4-hour, 6-hour, and 8-hour guided trips. Kids and novices are welcome and multi-boat parties are available. Transportation is easy and all tackle is furnished. https://www.orlandobass.com/

-LAKE GEORGE is the second largest lake in Florida and a natural lake from the St. Johns River.

-LAKE TOHO is located in Osceola County and holds the distinction of the top five largest five fish bags in bass fishing tournaments. As well as the all-time heaviest one day catch list.

Check out the internet for some of the websites that list the Florida bass fishing guides and give them a call. There are also thousands of lodging company websites that can show you the highs of any trip to Florida. You can just type in the location specific keywords of the place you'd like to visit to any search engine along with "lodge," "resort," or even "fish camp." and see how a weekend or a week of Florida bass fishing could provide adventure for you and your family. This is one experience you're likely to never forget.

An Adventure for the Whole Family

Bass fishing is one of America's top pastimes. Many people indulge in this activity for its therapeutic wonders. Great relaxation and the exhilarating feeling of catching a big bass is its biggest drawing power. Many memorable times are experienced between friends and family on these bass fishing trips.

Not all states are blessed with having great places to go bass fishing. Residents of Florida, though, have a great reason to be happy because they are one of the states in America that do have many places to fish and they capitalize on it. In fact, many of these lakes are transformed to wonderful bass fishing trip destinations.

Many of them have been developed and provided with lodging and rental establishments to cater to the needs of the bass fishermen. Aside from that, there are also many interesting side trips you can take your family to.

Southwest Florida has already acquired worldwide recognition for its exceptionally rich saltwater fishing, but its freshwater fishing could never be forgotten by anyone who has tried the bass fishing opportunities there.

Local residents are brought together by a series of regular competitions organized by three very active freshwater clubs in Collier County. There are also some open competitions that can be enjoyed by out of town fishermen. They can either compete or just plain watch the excitement going on as a spectator. Friendly tournaments are a great common focus of all of these clubs.

The state of Florida is blessed with beautiful and rich lakes that are great freshwater fishing. This could be enjoyed throughout all of the southwest regions. There are also ponds, canals, and creeks in other places that have good numbers of bass contained therein.

There are lodging businesses created to provide information and invitations for bass loving aficionados to come, sample, and prove that not all big fish are caught by professional fishermen.

These companies provide great details on what you will discover and experience in Florida when you go there. They center on the bass fishing aspect of the trip and also the other activities you can do while being there. They also would help you plan your trip and set up an itinerary.

The resort owners and the local tourist boards create most of these websites. They provide services as well as packages for either a small or large group. They will provide you with all the information you may need about bass fishing in Florida.

For those just starting out in bass fishing, Florida has some of the best bass fishermen to help you, teach you, and share some of their experienced tips. They know all the best spots to go to and the best gear to use.

One of these places is Lake Kissimmee in Central Florida. Experience the thrill of fishing for giant lunker largemouth bass in this famous lake resort. They have comfortable lodgings as well as great rentals for anyone who wants to try to catch a big one.

Aside from that, Lake Kissimmee is just a stone's throw away from Walt Disney World, Sea World, Universal Studios, and the metropolitan Orlando area. This means that even the kids can enjoy the other aspects of this bass fishing trip in Florida. You will see and enjoy a Florida getaway adventure everyone would like to have in his or her lifetime.

Aside from the Kissimmee chain of Lakes, you can go to Farm 13/Stickmarsh, Blue Cypress, and Walk-in-Water any time for more bass fishing. The famous Indian River Lagoon offers fishing for Redfish, Snook, Trout, and Tarpon aside from bass fishing. You can get a variety of catches in both fresh and saltwater.

Bass Fishing in Central Florida

Fishing in central Florida is easy, exciting, and fun because there are so many productive places to fish in this part of the state. You can pull off to the side of the road nearly anywhere as it's just expected that people will be fishing almost any body of water. It's not stretching the truth to say that if you see some water and it's more than a few inches deep, there's probably fish to be caught. Pair this with the fantastic weather central Florida has and you've got heaven on earth for many bass fishermen. You can go bass fishing almost every day.

You can possibly fish every day of the year and that adds to the attraction as a fishing Mecca. Your chances of catching what you want can vary with the time of the year, but with the temperature and weather barely fluctuating, it is very likely to catch a fish even when "out of season."

Central Florida offers not only Lake Toho, which is the most popular lake of the Kissimmee chain, but the famed Stick Marsh-Farm 13 fishery as well as the trophy bass lake, Walk in Water. Lake Toho is relatively shallow 18,800 acre lake that is covered with various types of aquatic vegetation. The most abundant is the massive hydrilla beds that can be found growing to the surface in up to 12 feet of water.

For Florida bass fishing, bream fishing, or anything in between, Bass World Lodge is the place to be http://www.bassworldlodge.net. Their location on the St. Johns River in Crescent City, Florida gives you quick access to some of the most productive Florida bass fishing grounds in the United States. Bass World Lodge offers professional guide services, spacious cabins, and fully stocked bait and tackle shops as well as bass and pontoon boat rentals.

Lake Toho is a lake that runs north/south and the lake is approximately nine miles long by only a couple miles wide.

Similar to most of the Florida lakes, medium to large wild shiners are the best producers for trophy fish. However, many lunkers are taken on soft plastics, Carolina rigs, rat-L-traps, crank baits, and soft plastic jerk baits. Suspending hard plastic jerk baits are one of the favorites of local fishermen.

Because the St. Johns river flows north, the upper basin is the area to the south that forms its marshy headwaters. The middle basin is the area in central Florida where the river widens forming lakes Harney, Jessup, Monroe, and George. The lower basin is the area in northeast Florida from Putnam County to the river's mouth in Duval County.

The source of the river, or headwaters, is a large marshy area in Indian River County. It flows north and turns eastward at Jacksonville to its mouth which empties into the Atlantic Ocean

The total drop of the river from its source in swamps south of Melbourne to its mouth in the Atlantic near Jacksonville is less than 30 feet, or about one inch per mile, making it one of the "laziest" rivers in the world. Because the river flows slowly, it is difficult to flush pollutants.

For example, the water color in the Harris Chain is quite stained. This is a blessing as most bass in these lakes are shallow and hold close to cover. Noisy lures are effective and multiple presentations to the same spot are required to get the fish's attention.

The biggest problem most fisherman encounter when fishing in the Harris chain for the first time is purely mental. Coming from other areas of the state or country, they look at the pea-soup water color and get the impression that these lakes are fishless. This is a shame as they are missing out on some great action if they only knew more about fishing under these conditions. Never underestimate central Florida for bass.

When you go fishing from one place to another in the U.S., you will see many different types of lakes and rivers. Each body of water has its own endearing characteristic but they also have a lot of things in common. And that is where the lakes and rivers in central Florida differ from all the other lakes in the United States, they seem to have their own uniqueness.

It is popularly known that central Florida is famous for fantastic bass fishing. They have the best lakes in the entire state because they have the finest largemouth bass any other lakes could produce.

Bass fishing in central Florida is world class throughout the year. The reproduction of this fish occurs between December and April at which time the bass will be at their heaviest. Eight to ten pound trophy-class fish are possible on any given day, with a chance at even larger bass all the time.

Now, it's time for you to start the ultimate fishing trip. But where in central Florida can you can catch these fish. Here is a list of lakes where you can find the best bass fishing in all of central Florida.

-Lake Tohopekiga or "Lake Toho", Florida's trophy largemouth fisheries are found in there. It is actually one of the places where B.A.S.S. tournaments are held. This area is also known as the Kissimmee chain of lakes.

-Lake Cypress

-Lake Kissimmee

-Lake Okeechobee

-And others we will discuss shortly

Try to visit these lakes and you will never regret it. While there are so many seasoned bass fishermen from central Florida and some from out of state, there are also those who have little or no experience just yet, but want to take up the sport. It is necessary to know that it is not just about throwing a line in the water and waiting. There are some necessary procedures and laws to follow.

The following are important guidelines for bass fishing in central Florida:

1. Be sure that the boats you are going to use are fully equipped with all U.S. Coast Guard safety equipment and take a cell phone for emergency purposes.

2. It is a must to consider the weather condition. You should leave the water when a storm comes or if there is lightning in the area. Florida is the lightning capital. Summer storms come up quickly and can be deadly.

3. You should start to fish early in the morning or in the evening because bass are more active at those times.

4. Bring extra rods and reels. You might need it. But, if you feel like you want the guide services to help you, many already offer all the equipment you need.

Different bass fishing guide agencies will assist you with your tour. They may charge you a certain amount, but it is an expense that will be worth it. You will love the experience that bass fishing here will give to you.

As a reminder, do not forget to bring with you your sunglasses and sunscreen because it might get hot out there. Wear a lot of light weight, long clothes and a hat for sun protection. And cover any remaining areas with plenty of sun block.

Columbia makes an excellent line of sun protection clothing specifically designed for fishing, P.F.G., Performance Fishing Gear. Sizes and styles are available for men and women.

Columbia Solar Camo water repellent, wicking material, and sun shade.

http://bit.ly/2awj6Jv

And, of course, do not forget to bring food and water. You don't want an angry stomach on your bass fishing trip, do you?

And best of all be sure you have your camera so you can take pictures as a memory of your fantastic fishing trip in central Florida, as well as that whopping 10 pounder that you might have caught.

Ocala Florida is a great place. If you want to make your fishing vacation more pleasant by remembering that it is a fishing vacation, make it a point that you are prepared to enjoy the whole experience, which includes kicking back and enjoying your friends, your surroundings, and your brief respite from the daily stresses of your life.

But some of the people who take a vacation do it to not only relax themselves from their stressful days, but they go for bass fishing for a purpose and a challenge. They may enter a tournament, which is a competition of big bass caught by many anglers competing against each other.

Before entering any bass fishing tournament in Florida try to remember some of these things.

The first step is to be sure that you have established your actual fishing goals, and then ensure that they are in fact realistic based on the amount of time you plan to spend seeking those goals and they align with the overall vision and purpose of the individual tournament.

The majority of bass fishermen will tell you that they are going to Florida seeking that elusive goal of catching a bass over ten pounds. If this is a goal you have considered, ask yourself how much time you will be able to spend in this endeavor. Fishing for a bass that size is what you have been doing since you started bass fishing; will eight hours on the water really give you that chance you are looking for? Maybe, maybe not. Although they may live in that body of water, in more numbers than your home waters, it still may take time to learn the water and score a big catch.

Your decision to hit the waters of Florida are a step in the right direction, but remember that fishing is fishing. Can you realistically expect to get it done in an eight hour day? Sounds easy but the truth is, it's not. In a tournament situation, it may prove more enjoyable to take in the whole experience and enjoy the competition and making more friends rather than unrealistic expectations of a big catch.

The Florida Fish and Wildlife Conservation Commission (FWC) makes a list each year of what they consider to be among the top ten bass lakes, which will give you a starting point. This list is based on both shock surveys and creel counts that are reported by fishermen during creel surveys.

You now need to narrow the list down to your selection and the only way to do this realistically is to get several references based on other people's experiences. This is where they usually hold the tournaments. Ocala, Florida rarely leaves that list.

More information on notable central Florida lakes:

Lake George

Lake George is one of the premier largemouth bass fishing lakes in Florida. It is the second largest lake in the state (46,000 acres) and is 18 miles northwest of Deland and 29 miles east of Ocala.

Lake George is one of the many natural lakes on the St. Johns River. It has extensive vegetation that provides excellent habitat for bass. Fishing in eelgrass with plastic worms fished in and around the vegetation, and top water artificial lures are productive. Fishing with live shiners is an excellent method for catching trophy bass during the spring spawning season.

Hot spots on the lake include Juniper Springs Run, Salt Springs Run, and Silver Glen Springs Run on the western shoreline. In winter and early spring, look for bass to congregate at the jetties on the south end of the lake. Casting deep-diving crank baits near old dock structures along the northeast shore and off Drayton Island can also be productive.

Stick Marsh/Farm 13 Reservoir

Created in 1987, the Farm 13/Stick Marsh Reservoir is synonymous with trophy bass fishing. This 6,500-acre reservoir near Fellsmere, west of Vero Beach, became one of the hottest bass lakes in the country during the past decade. FWC biologists predict a continuation of excellent largemouth bass fishing in upcoming years. Electrofishing samples continue to indicate good reproduction and growth of bass in the reservoir.

Anglers can locate bass throughout the reservoir among a variety of habitats, including woody stump fields, submerged canals, and hydrilla. Summer 2004 hurricanes drastically reduced levels of hydrilla throughout the reservoir, which can affect where the bass are located. Anglers should keep this in mind when trying to pattern fish. Plastic worms, spinner baits, crank baits, soft jerk baits, and top water propeller baits are effective. Wild golden shiners are the top choice for anglers looking to catch a trophy fish.

The recreational harvest regulation for largemouth bass anglers is catch-and-release. There is a two-lane boat ramp, paved parking lot, picnic pavilions, and restrooms. No gasoline, food, ice or other facilities are available on site. This area is part of the St. Johns Blue Cypress Management Unit. See here for a recreational map of that unit. http://www.sjrwmd.com/recreationguide/maps/Blue_Cypress_Conservation_Area.pdf

These are some of the lakes where tournaments have been held and could be the place where future tournaments can be done. Try to practice and study the area so that when tournament time comes, you have an edge over the competition.

The St. Johns River

Good freshwater fishing can be found not only in lakes but also in rivers, ponds, creeks, and canals. St. Johns River is the longest river in Florida. Its clear copper-colored waters and floating hyacinth islands are bold and enchanting. The area contains marshy wetlands as well as citrus groves which are irrigated by zigzag canals linking the reservoirs, swamps, lakes, palm trees, flat-water marshes and cypress stands.

Large numbers of the best and the biggest trophy black bass are caught on a regular basis. Wetland-dependent species thrive here including blue herons, limpkins, pelicans, turkey, alligators, bald eagles, rabbits, wild hogs, tortoise, deer, wood storks, populous, and ospreys.

The river itself is great for fishing and catching enormous sizes of fish. In order to fish for bass in rivers, it is sometimes best to seek out breaks in the current, perhaps from a fallen tree, a stump, or rocks. Some kind of structure or cover they can relate to. If there isn't structure or cover, look for irregularities of the bottom. Even a shade line can be enough to hold fish. The fish that bass feed upon will normally school below a dam, thereby making these spots ideal for bass fishing. There are numerous techniques available to pursue these fish.

For a beginner, it is advised to gather more basic tools to get started. Both amateur and seasoned anglers use spinning equipment especially in Florida. More seasoned bass fishermen like a lot of baitcasting gear.

Ditches and dikes were constructed in the St. John's River headwaters in order to serve agricultural pursuits. To expose rich soils to grow citrus, row crops, and to raise beef cattle, the marshes were drained.

However, channeling the St. John's headwaters for groves, farms, and ranches eliminated hundreds of thousands of acres of marshes, which upset the fragile wetlands ecology that was the foraging, nesting and nursery habitat for wildlife. It made the area susceptible to damage from the floods created by hurricanes.

In 1988, the Management District and the US Army Corps of Engineers began a project to restore the drained marshes, construct reservoirs, levees, canals, spillways, and water control structures to provide flood protection to the area. The project also created some fantastic trophy bass fisheries. Since then more than 150,000 acres of marshes are being restored and enhanced in the Upper St. John's River headwaters reclamation project.

People all over the world come and visit Florida, not just because of its natural beauty, but because of its spectacular bass fishing and adventure.

Lake Okeechobee and The Everglades

Okeechobee is a Seminole Indian word loosely meaning "big water." True to its name, Lake Okeechobee is 730 square miles in size. It is the greatest provider of drinking water for south Florida, averaging 9 feet in depth up to a maximum of 17 feet deep. Lake Okeechobee is in Glades, Okeechobee, Martin, Palm Beach, and Hendry Counties. Recharge comes from precipitation and southward flow of water from the Kissimmee River. Historically, hydro pattern flowed southward over millions of acres into the Everglades.

It is the second largest freshwater lake in the United States after Lake Michigan and its fishing reputation matches its size. Much of the lake's 730 square miles or 450,000 acres are hidden from view by a dyke, levee, or trees that screen the shore.

Lake Okeechobee has a 150 mile circumference and its invisible opposite shore is more than 30 miles away. The best fishing and more than half of the action takes place along the lake's western shore.

Lake Okeechobee links the Atlantic and Gulf sides of Florida via the Port Mayaca Lock on the east side of the lake and the Moore Haven Lock on the lake's western side. Drainage canals lower the lake and drain adjacent lands for farming. Agricultural activities around the Lake Okeechobee area include cattle ranching, dairy farming, and crop production of sugarcane, winter vegetables, citrus, sod, sweet corn, and rice. This many players and interests in the area often contributes to ongoing political disputes and water resource management conflicts. Hoover Dike was constructed along the southern regions of Lake Okeechobee to prevent flooding while also yielding year-round crop production. Tory mucks of the region contain 50 percent or more mineral matter by weight and have considerably more native fertility than sawgrass mucks, which were formed under logographic conditions.

The 1950s were a period of technological ambition and construction, a system of canals, dikes, and pumping stations were installed to distribute water to the Everglades agricultural areas from Lake Okeechobee. To this day, water flow, pollution, and rights are a hot political issue concerning many different parties and viewpoints.

Florida's Lake Okeechobee is one of the most famous big bass lakes in the country for many years. It been noted by some that it has produces the best largemouth bass, bluegill, and speck (crappie) fishing in the world.

Roland Martin's Marina on Lake Okeechobee has been one of the top bass fishing destinations in the world since they opened their doors in 1981. They have built their reputation on years of providing customer satisfaction and still continue to set the standard in the fishing industry. The group of Florida fishing guides there are noted to be the "Best of the Best" when it comes to fishing Lake Okeechobee or the Florida Everglades.

They have been considered some of Florida's most credible guides. They have been featured on ESPN2, TNN, OLN, FSN, and the OUTDOOR CHANNEL. They are the best whenever you plan to go fishing in south central Florida on Lake Okeechobee or the Florida Everglades. They ensure that the customers will have no regrets at the end of the day.

On Lake Okeechobee the two effective ways to catch largemouth bass are either with artificial lures or wild shiners. Bass fishing with wild shiners on Lake Okeechobee has been one of the most popular methods for catching bass, especially for the trophy bass. Fishing with a wild shiner can be a very fast-paced way of catching bass. When you get on them, you won't have time to do much else other than set the hook.

On the other hand, bass fishing with artificial lures is the other great way to catch bass on Lake Okeechobee. The guides will provide you with a choice between spinning or baitcasting reels. The methods of either flipping or pitching are a very effective way to catch bass on Lake Okeechobee as well as other techniques we'll get to shortly.

Lake Okeechobee fishing is well-known not only throughout the U.S. but the whole world. Some guide services have clients who come from all over the world, including Japan and Europe, just to fish Lake Okeechobee.

Lake Okeechobee guides provide trips and tours that are all conducted by highly trained and efficient guides. They know the movement of the fish and their feeding patterns, which gives you the best advantage over the fish and landing the lunker of a lifetime. Their hospitable manner and willingness to help you enjoy your day on the water is genuine. Whether you want to book a corporate trip, take a youngster fishing for the first time, or have special needs, they are there to help. As a tourist, there are advantages in terms of service and hospitality from one of the most prestigious Florida bass fishing guide services.

If you want to go it alone, Lake Okeechobee is heavily ringed with tackle shops, marinas, motels, restaurants, etc. You can find rental boats, gear, and lodging to make your bass fishing trip more convenient and comfortable.

The lake offers all types of waterway structures to fish from open water to narrow canals surrounded by hundreds of different types of vegetation and grasses.

The lake is approximately 37 miles long by 30 miles wide. To fishermen nationwide, it's renowned for the number of bass it contains per acre and that it also produces more bass over 7 pounds than any lake in Florida and the United States. Those stats make for good odds while fishing.

Fishing at Lake Okeechobee for bass from late fall to early spring is when crappie and bass fishing is at its best. Success comes when using large wild shiners or artificial lures of all types. If you want to target a true monster size bass, fishing at Lake O is certainly the way to go.

The Everglades

Okeechobee is also the gatekeeper to the Everglades. Most anglers agree that bass fishing in the Everglades is a unique and captivating experience. Many people visit this unique environment expecting the stereotypical swamplands of old movies. What they find is one of the country's most extraordinary natural formations. Thousands of kinds of fish, dozens of endangered species, and land forms unlike anywhere else in the United States can all be found in the Everglades. These surroundings also provide some of the best largemouth bass waters in the country. However, anyone who spends time bass fishing in the Everglades will discover more than just an angling adventure.

In a park that boasts more than one million acres of natural terrain and two thousand miles of canals along with a whole lot of alligators, the visiting fisherman might be wise to take along a professional guide or a buddy. Enlisting an experienced local for bass fishing in the Everglades can make the trip more enjoyable and productive as well as less dangerous. In addition, employing a guide means a visitor to Florida doesn't have to personally purchase a state fishing license. He/she fishes under the auspices of the guide's licenses. A licensed guide will soon have a bass fisherman just where he/she wants to be, navigating the channels in search of the lushly vegetated flats where literally hundreds of hungry bass are looking for dinner.

Once on the water, even the novice fisherman will find that casting a line generally results in hits not just from trophy size largemouth but from feisty exotic species as well. Largemouth bass over fifteen inches long and weighing in at more than a few pounds are not uncommon in Everglade waters. Anglers who like a good fight will get it from the largemouth's hard fighting cousin by name, the peacock bass. Although the park strongly encourages catch and release an enthusiastic angler won't go home without a memento of the visit. Remember all a taxidermist needs to provide a conversation piece wall hanging are the dimensions of the fish and a good picture. Do the Everglades a favor, handle that bass with care and don't take more than a fair share of any fish wherever you go.

Also beware of the extreme temperatures which can decrease the pleasure and lower the productivity of any bass fishing in the Everglades. Consider early morning and dusk fishing when the waters are cooler, more oxygenated and livelier. Be sure to dress for success, lightweight shorts or pants, heat gear, vented shirts, billed caps, polarized sunglasses, bug spray, and lots of sunscreen are de rigueur.

All in all, for the fisherman looking for a one of a kind trip, bass fishing in the Everglades may be just the ticket. So, get in touch with a guide, pack up the gear, don't forget the sunglasses, and head out today for one of the nation's true natural wonderlands, The Florida Everglades.

Urban Bass Fishing

When most people think of fishing in Florida, they think of the coastal and offshore opportunities. If you mention bass fishing, they probably think of a nice lake or pond surrounded by palm trees. But, an often unknown and forgotten Florida fishing opportunity is the urban canal system.

The Southern Florida counties of Palm Beach, Broward, and Miami-Dade contain a system of man-made urban canals that can harbor some large fish. They were constructed in the early 1900's for drainage and flood protection. They are freshwater canals and contain rocky limestone sides and bottom with some vegetation growing in many areas. They are cross cut in long skinny canals that intersect at various places creating a latticework of waterways for you to explore and fish. Many are continually filled with freshwater from the underground aquifer creating a very clear water environment. And not to mention the experience of seeing all the wildlife that inhabits the canal system even in the most urban environments.

You can fish from the bank, drop a canoe or kayak in almost anywhere, or launch from one of the listed boat ramps the FWC lists on their site. A couple of my favorites are Snapper Creek and Black Creek canals.
http://myfwc.com/fishing/freshwater/sites-forecast/s/metropolitan-miami-canals/

The FWC also maintains a list of guides, tackle shops, and taxidermists right on that page. The canal system, in my opinion, offers a better chance for solo fishing as opposed to finding hot spots by chance in a gigantic lake. You can park your car along the road and with a little bit of gear, theoretically, walk miles of canals and cover a lot of water. That will increase your chances of hitting a honey hole.

You'll find largemouth bass along the sides of the canals, holding under vegetation or structure, and at the intersections of canals. Top water and faster moving baits, due to the clarity of some of the waters, will likely yield success. Frogs, soft or hard jerkbaits, swimbaits, and grubs should all produce fish. There should be lots of bank fishing opportunity. There is even lots of room to fly fish from shore. Just be mindful of not venturing onto private property accidentally.

As a bonus and a by catch, you may encounter some other exciting species in addition to bass. Other species may include saltwater species in the canals without obstruction leading to saltwater. They may also be more fresh or brackish water tolerant. Here you may find snook or even tarpon. Other freshwater species inside of the water control devices include Mayan cichlids, jaguar capote, oscars, and snakeheads. Lastly, of course, there is the peacock bass that resides in the canals.

Peacock Bass Fishing

Along with the great surge of interest of the people with bass fishing in the entire state, comes another kind of freshwater fish which has vigorous physical strength. Open yourself up to the interesting world of peacock bass fishing.

A peacock bass is actually from the cichlid family of fish not from the bass family, though its body shape resembles that of a largemouth bass in many ways. This fish has only been in South Florida since 1984. We are the first generation of fishermen who get to experience hunting and catching this exotic species. It is only able to survive the Winters in the South Florida canal system due to the aquifer a few feet below the canals which seeps warm water into the waterway year round. They were introduced in order to check the population of other exotic species of fish found in the canal system. In any case, this presents anglers a unique opportunity to catch a beautiful and exotic fish in an urban environment. Many times, they can be caught from the bank and a boat is not required.

Unlike its North American counterpart, the largemouth, the peacock bass is a lot more eye-appealing and vibrantly decorated with the various shades of green, blue, orange and gold like the one in the picture above caught in the Black Creek Canal at 97th st. in Miami. But, we should not be taken in by this dazzling facade because, as a matter of fact, they are far more aggressive than the largemouths. They can break you off or destroy the tackle that would already be enough to restrain the toughest of largemouths.

One more difference which can be observed is that the largest among largemouth are always the female while in peacock bass, either the male or the female can grow to a large size.

The peacock bass is generally categorized into four distinct species: (a) the speckled peacock, (b) the peacock (c) the butterfly peacock, and (d) the royal peacock. Fish biologists still suggest that various other types may actually be present in South America.

It may have acquired its name from the fact that the spot, a black circular "eye spot" which is notably rimmed in gold, on the base of the caudal fin which bears a close resemblance to the tail plume of a peacock fowl.

Male peacocks are normally described to have a well-known hump on their head which could be used as a battering ram in battles with other males and to protect the fry and their territory as well. Some believe that the hump may be a fat deposit that the male peacock uses to nourish himself when he is not feeding. Perhaps it is both.

It should be noted that before you indulge in the activity you should prepare everything that would be needed at first. You can log on to the web, read magazines or other activity if we want detailed information about this type of fishing in addition to this book. Consultations may be done online with friends, forum members, and pros so we could be provided with a lot of options to choose from. It would serve as your guide on what you are going to bring, basically, on what you are going to need when you go peacock bass fishing.

You should also not fail to notice the tips that expert fishermen have, especially for beginners because this would literally be a world of help aside from having a guide during the activity. It's better that you already have something in your mind about what's going to happen in order that you'll be able to assess whether you can do it or not. And since it is a fact that peacock bass fishing somewhat requires physical endurance it would be better to train your body long before the activity. You may be walking long distances, down uneven or unstable banks, and in blazing hot sun and humidity for hours at a time. If that seems unreasonable, consult a guide or consider another mode of fishing.

When I think of fishing for peacock bass, I immediately think of Hai Truong. For south Florida peacocks, largemouths, and other exotic species, Hai Truong is the guide to call. Trips can be booked here.
http://www.haitruongfishing.com/services.html

This activity is unquestionably one that will offer us great fun and that you'll surely stop thinking about your worries even if just for a couple of hours. We often times disregard the fact that we should give ourselves a break after having worked hard to give our minds a time to refresh our thoughts and our body a chance to relax and recharge. Urban fishing is a quick and effective way to do that in an enjoyable setting.

The challenge that is offered when catching an unruly peacock bass and the memories that you'll have with your fellow adventure seekers will certainly linger for a long time to come.

The only way to keep up with the latest about peacock bass fishing is to constantly stay on the lookout for new information and put in your time on the water. If you read everything you find about peacock bass fishing, and try to implement it on the water yourself, it won't take long for you to become a proficient angler for this exciting species.

Now that we've covered those aspects of peacock bass fishing, let's turn to some of the other factors that need to be considered.

Peacock bass fishing is one of the most adventurous targets for the sport fishing game in the world. What makes it difficult for untrained sport fishermen to venture in without knowledge and be successful?

Peacock bass fish have earned a reputation in the bass fishing world as ferocious, very powerful, and a bad-tempered sport fish. It behaves like a largemouth bass on steroids, which makes it difficult for anglers to catch. Once it decides to hit the lure, unsuspicious anglers are shocked because it strikes with such power, dragging away the bait without being caught by the fishermen. This happened to me my first time. I broke off a big one. My leader wasn't sufficient. My knot was probably suspect. My drag wasn't set right. On many fronts, I was just lazy and not really prepared for the fish I could encounter.

Its strength is estimated to be twice or more from other largemouth. Many sport fishermen do think that a minute or two of fighting with this large bass-looking fish will make them tired easily, but their presumption is not accurate. Peacock bass usually have another shot of bursting power, thus it is not always as easy as catching a regular bass.

Biological studies show what a peacock bass is and why it is different to other fish. They are members of the cichlids, which are reputed to be one of the most highly evolved group of fishes. Peacock bass are often classified as a predator, which feeds entirely on small bait fish.

It is usually found in the rivers of South America and the Amazon, but some make their home here in Florida thanks to the state agencies who introduced them. Its speed, strength, size, and ferocious nature make it easy to hunt for their prey. Similarly, to a largemouth bass with huge, bucket-like mouth, peacock bass do swallow up other fish of smaller sizes for their meal.

One of the strategies of success in pursuing a peacock bass is the mastering of the fishing technique in relation to the behavior of the fish. It is advised to at least improve some on everything an angler knows. They must also take into consideration the biological history of the fish to come up with new techniques and become familiar with south Florida's weather, where the peacock bass is found. And from this, determine the best season for hunting it. They prefer baitfish imitating lures. A handy tip to keep in mind on your first outing.

Lastly, the fishing gear such as rods, reels, and baits must be wisely selected in order to cope with the style of the peacock bass. When everything is set up and ready, the next question is, can you survive a wild peacock bass fishing adventure?

Now you know a little bit about peacock bass fishing. Even if you don't know everything, you've done something worthwhile: you've expanded your knowledge and targeted, and hopefully will catch a beautiful fish few other people get a chance to.

Finding the Fish

Before you go out fishing, if you're not going with a guide, you'll want to do some research on the local area. Going out to a big body of water can be daunting if you've never been there before and there are no signs readily apparent that fish are anywhere nearby. Before you go, do a search online for the area and body of water you'll be fishing. Chances are, some fishing reports and youtube videos will come up. Use this intelligence to your advantage. Here's a tip, in your search, include the month you are fishing. Many times, a report contains the time of year which is a more specific variable wise regarding the patterns the fish are most likely to respond to at that time. These reports will include lots of details about time of year, time of day, wind, sun, current, moon phase, tides (if applicable), lures, and techniques used. If you're lucky, you may get exact locations. Use this information as a starting point to formulate a plan for the day.

In the search results, you're also likely to find archived fishing forum discussions. If these are public, you can often glean more good intelligence, launch points, and techniques to use in certain areas. These are discussions among locals about specific areas and what is working. It can be a wealth of information in an environment where people are willing to give up their most hard earned knowledge.

And, be sure to check your local bait shop. As you purchase your gear, see if they have any current knowledge on good places to try and what the fish are biting on recently. Don't expect someone's secret honey hole, but the bait dealer, after patronizing his/her business is likely to offer up some good help in order for you to be successful out there.

Bass are fighters, they are elusive, a predator by nature, and a prized catch, of many an aspiring angler. You can catch bigger fish, more often, and in more places by having a proactive plan and approach, stacking the odds in your favor of success. Catching more fish and enjoying the process, is what this basic guide is all about.

Start thinking like the bass as a predator. Understand the bass as a hunter and opportunist. Observe, learn, follow, and study them. Use its natural habits, preferences, patterns, and prey, in your angling strategy. You will have some interesting fish stories to tell. And you'll learn the most from the ones that get away.

It's true, no matter what the context, body of water, situation or condition, regardless of secrets, tips, science, or techniques, bass fishing in Florida is challenging and rewarding at the same time. To ensure hours of enjoyment, follow the pointers provided here for fishing and always be anticipating the next bite.

There are various aspects working in combination in the art, science, and sport that is fishing. Strategy and synergy, contribute to eventual consistent and repeatable success. Equipment, location, lures, dawn and or dusk, shallow or deep waters, it doesn't matter. There are techniques for each of them. There are always many variables at work. In the end, it is as much about the process, enjoyment, and appreciation, as it is about the fish.

If you have more time in an area, or if you live in Florida, rather than just a few days of vacation, look at it as an ongoing process and journey. Every time you go out to the same body of water, your greatest weapon is what you learned the last time you were there. Do so using all to your advantage as you undertake your own journey.

Various scientists have shown that bass almost calculate the amount of energy it will take them to go after the prey vs. the return. If this is true and verified, what are the implications for us anglers? Outsmarting them, of course. It's all in the basics, the strategies, battle plan, and techniques we choose to use in this process. This will dictate and determine our success.

It is said that 90% of the fish are in 10% of the water. Going out onto a body of water and blindly casting probably isn't going to be successful. Sure, you'll get lucky by random chance a few times, but it would be much better to get, at least, some idea of where to go where fish might be *likely* to be. How can you know this if you've never been to an area before or are new to it?

Nothing could be said here that will be correct 100% of the time given the vast area and bodies of water we all will be fishing. Read up or watch videos on the local area you'll be fishing. When I've looked for new places to fish, not only did I want to know where to put my boat in, but I wanted to know what kind of fish are there, which way to go, what techniques/lures to use, and what spots to fish specifically. And then coordinate this with what the wind, weather, tides, etc. is supposed to do that day. Through several articles and a couple of Youtube videos, I was able to get a pretty good idea of the strategy I was going to employ when I got there. This can allow you to get a leg up knowledge wise without having to go out and learn it all from scratch aimlessly by yourself.

If you're lacking information, you can gather it yourself. Usually, the night before a trip, as you're getting lures and rods ready, or maybe filing a float plan, you can spend about 20 or 30 mins checking out the maps of the area. There may be fishing or navigational maps available in local stores in the area, but Google, Yahoo, Bing, and MapQuest all offer aerial view map features that just might clue you into good spots to fish like points, humps, deep holes, channels, docks, or subsurface structure or cover.

You can use the road map feature to find routes to your launch sites and park land shown in green. And you can use the satellite feature to determine the good areas near banks, on points, or subsurface to find fish hiding spots.

https://www.google.com/maps

Know your area as best you can *before* you go. That's the best and quickest way to at least end up in the vicinity of where fish might be that day. Look for any irregularities from rock piles, to ledges, to other man-made structures. Fish will usually relate to those things through most of the year. Look for spawning fish in shallows in the spring. Fish do move from time to time and throughout the day according to conditions. Locating them is the first step. From there, you can start your patterning of the fish and what lures to use for that day.

Must Have Tackle for Florida Waters

You'll need to equip yourself with some of the necessary bass fishing equipment if you're to land a big one in Florida waters.

Rod Selection

There isn't a more important tool for accomplishing your goal of catching more fish (other than a boat) than the fishing rod, itself.

To me, a good all-purpose design for freshwater bass fishing in Florida might look something like this:

- A reasonable length handle for casting leverage, but not so long as to interfere with retrieval techniques
- Split foam or cork handle
- Light weight
- Balanced
- Medium to medium heavy power-For sensitivity and pulling largemouth bass out of heavy cover or matted vegetation or strong fighting peacocks
- 6' to 7'-For casting small lures a long distance
- 1/8 – ½ oz. bait weight range
- 8 – 20# line rating. Up to 60# braid can be used
- Spinning and/or baitcasting option

The rod specifications should cover several different rod types and fishing techniques you'll need to do battle in the environment you find yourself in in Florida. I'll have other technique specific rods including a seven foot, medium-light, fast action small jig rod. And a seven foot, medium, moderate action, swimbait/crankbait rod to name a few.

The more moderate action of a swimbait/crankbait rod will help you in keeping the fish on during the fight. Fish can often use leverage to unhook themselves. The more forgiving nature of a moderate action shaft keeps the treble hooks embedded in the fish's mouth instead of having something more rigid to gain leverage on like a faster action rod and non-stretchable braided line.

Sometimes, you may encounter a paradox or compromise of sorts. A suspending jerkbait has treble hooks. Do you go with the moderate action rod to keep the fish on during the fight? Or do you go with the faster action to be able to impart the darting, slashing, walking action on the lures to get the fish to bite in the first place. You can see how you can't do both at the same time.

In this case, we usually opt for the fast action rod, with non-stretch braided line to be able to impart the needed action on the lure. It's probably more important that your presentation is correct. Without that, there won't be any fish caught to land in the first place. So you attempt to land the fish even though he may have slightly more advantage now with a stiffer rod and small treble hooks.

Of course, there is always the option of replacing your treble hooks with single hooks. That way, you won't get hung up on as much vegetation in Florida waters and your rod will be better suited to fighting and actually landing the fish with that type of hook.

Having the right equipment, knowing how to best use it, when and how, (also how not to use it and what it is not suitable for), can all help you in your bass fishing adventure.

The basics regarding rods, reels, line, hooks, weights, bobbers, sinkers, lures, and other equipment (hats, PFD's, nets, scents, scissors etc.), gives you an appreciation for having the right tools for the task(s) at hand.

As a highly participatory and engaging sport, fishing is simply almost unparalleled in the vast amount of styles and tools to use. From quiet streams, tranquil lakes to open water and rushing rivers, there is something for everyone.

If you are looking for quick tips on the right equipment, most suited to your purpose and the techniques to master to catch bass in any conditions, let this next section enlighten and inspire you, as you delve right into the utilities of the fishing trade.

Limited space does not permit large comparative explanations or ramblings on the merit of some tools above certain others. These debates are well known and well published in existing literature. We take a more practical approach and look at what you will actually need to hook your next fish, besides random chance and luck. We like to point out that picking the right equipment means a lot of different things to different people. Each angler has his/her own interpretation of what that means, varying skill level, physical characteristics, budgets, and strengths/weaknesses. So we will not profess knowing what is right for you. What we do offer are mere suggestions on which tools will stack the odds in your favor and help you enjoy preparing, rigging, baiting, hooking, retrieving and landing your next big one. Ensuring that it does not join the droves of the one that got away.

As you explore your surroundings and the wonder of fish species and their life cycles, patterns, and behavior, experimenting, hands-on with your equipment, and what is available to anglers today, is part of the exciting world of fishing. From fish-finders, temperature gauges, sensors, and more advanced technologies, to the art of preparing your lines and hooks, choosing the lures most suited to your circumstance and purpose and more, adds to the excitement and enjoyment of the activity. Preparing yourself with knowledge on these, will boost your confidence and practicing often, will pay off in the long run as your expertise, exposure and angling mastery grows.

When it comes to equipment, the opinions are many. Your conditions, circumstances, purpose, and goal will all figure into the final choice. Oh, and do not forget the ever-present budget and affordability.

Spinning or baitcasting with artificial lures, fly-fishing, trolling, are all options available to you, with specialist tools on hand to assist you in making the most of it. Typically a 6.5 to 7 feet rod (spinning or baitcasting), with a matching reel with six to ten pound line, fast action, would serve you well. Weedless hooks or rigs are a lifesaver in very dense cover or weeds.

Angling techniques and tackle keep refining, developing, and almost takes on a life of their own for every angler. There is not really a one-size-fits-all approach. This personalized relationship with your equipment, might mean a basic rod to start with and then adding a couple specialized ones for your different excursions and expeditions. Modern tackle and methods, traditional or innovative, technology-driven, whatever your fancy or preference, there is something for every taste and budget.

Most beginners might be overwhelmed by the selection of equipment available on the market today. Knowing what to pick and buy, how and when to apply, how to use it correctly, how to maximize your chances of success is key.

Good quality tackle is important. It needs to be adequate for whatever nature throws your way. You will need to build your arsenal of knowledge and equipment over time, to respond best to some of the challenges at hand. Good baits and lures and how to use them effectively, in combination, maybe in quick succession, to ensure bites. As is the importance of preparing, presenting well, accurate casting, setting the hook, as well as retrieving and landing of the fish.

All we will say, is that having expensive or the right equipment, is not a guarantee that you will land any fish. In fishing, there are no real guarantees. This is an activity between you and nature. Exploring and getting you to the point where you know the feel, function, and integral strengths and weaknesses of your equipment, is the real way to wisdom. For most trial and error, practice, and persistence are the routes to follow to becoming well-versed and experienced anglers.

Realizing the equipment's full potential will take time and practice. Bear in mind, that sophistication in equipment will develop in parallel to your own mastery and skill refinement.

Your intended style of fishing will dictate the most appropriate choice for tackle, boat, reel, rod, line, hooks, baits, lures, weights, sinkers, leaders, and more. There are rods, reels, line, hooks, leaders, baits, and landing tackle just right for any combination of those things.

Basic angling techniques are relatively easy to master, yet conquering and refining all the subtleties and intricate moves and maneuvers, exploring the secrets discovered, or yet to be discovered, will take a lifetime.

Practice and enjoy bass fishing, according to your own niche and style, preference, and location of choice. In a word, your "specialty." It is a very personalized and an individualized pursuit and passion. Always remember, that there is a wide array of variety and enjoyment on offer, by different kinds of fishing, locations, baits, and lures to keep angling interesting and a growing sport. It is contagious and pervasive. Once let in, it is hard to let go. You are hooked and being reeled in by this sport and hobby before you know it.

For most anglers, technique (and choice of equipment) is dictated by the species sought, established practice, conditions, and more. Mostly artificial lures are suggested and accepted for freshwater predatory fishing. Some prefer live bait, others have success with hard baits like crankbaits or poppers.

If you are fishing in weeds, heavy cover, thick, slop, grassy wetlands, swamps in Florida, a heavier line (braid) and heavier power rods will serve you better.

Apart from your own custom design, some of the most popular and in demand rods that have similar specifications are St. Croix fishing rods.

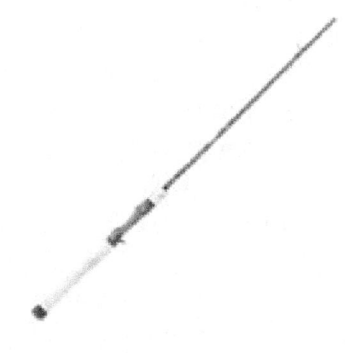

The St. Croix Legend Elite Casting Rod.

http://bit.ly/23EoWwX

The St. Croix Avid Series in casting or spinning.

http://bit.ly/1qoISVK

The St. Croix Premier Series in spinning or casting can be a very high quality rod that is matched with affordability.

http://bit.ly/1No8N5p

What may be the ultimate in affordability, durability, and performance, might be the Ugly Stick GX2 models in either spinning or casting versions. The price is attractive for any beginning or budgeted fisherman, but I really like that you can put the rod through hell and it's virtually indestructible. Even the guides have been replaced with no inserts so they don't pop out with such frequency. It's a good mix of fiberglass and graphite for lightness and sensitivity as well as durability. The seven foot, medium power, fast action should be applicable to many general freshwater fishing scenarios.

http://bit.ly/23uevzb

Reels

If given the opportunity to have a bad rod and a good reel or a good rod and a bad reel, I'd choose the good rod. The reel could be argued to be much less important. It could be a soda can on the other end of the line and all it has to do is wind it back in for you. Some anglers prefer certain brands or the manufacturing components of one reel over another. Some prefer how the drag operates. Or even the durability or corrosion resistance. Some like the lightness or smoothness of certain reels. I tend to prefer durability first. You can make your own decisions regarding which aspects of reels you like. But, many would agree that a good rod may take precedence over a high priced reel in most instances.

For normal bass fishing, spinning tackle, here too, we want to go as light as we can get away with. Even small, light-duty reels can land the occasional monster. As mine did when a big blue catfish hit my small spoon I was trolling.

A reel that is a 5.2:1 retrieve ratio and can hold six to 12 pound line is probably about right for a general freshwater spinning outfit.

Generally, Shimano, Diawa, Quantum, and Abu Garcia all make good spinning reels.

A higher level, quality spinning reel I like is the Quantum Smoke.

http://bit.ly/1Mu0nP3

A mid-level reliable spinning reel is something like the Abu Garcia Orra 2S.

http://bit.ly/1S6xcOZ

The Bass Pro Extreme spinning reel has some interesting design features and qualities; a larger spool for less line twist and casting distance, light, and smooth. And at a very attractive price point.

http://bit.ly/2bBxSy1

And some of the most durable reels ever made that are definitely on the lower end of the affordability spectrum are Mitchell reels. Like the Mitchell 300 series. My father still has old Mitchell reels that are older than I am and dinosaurs by today's standards, but still work and are likely to outlive us all.

http://bit.ly/1qoL0Nt

For casting reels, I prefer to have a 6.2:1 retrieve ratio reel for general duty, but also a 7.2:1 higher geared "burner" reel for faster retrieves of swimbaits and crankbaits. The lower geared reel allows you to use it, in combination with heavier line and heavier powered rods, to winch fish out of slop, cover, structure you may be fishing. If you try to do that with a higher geared reel, it won't work as well. It's like trying to get your manual transmission car rolling in fourth gear rather than first.

The numbers indicate how many spool turns to how many cranks of the reel handle. So 5 spool turns to every 1 crank of the handle is a faster retrieve than 4:1. This really has to do with speed versus power. The closer you are to 1:1, the more power it will have. The greater the difference between the two numbers, the more speed it will have.

A higher end bait caster reel that is light and low profile would be exemplified by the Shimano Curado low profile.

http://bit.ly/1N8odzP

Here too for a mid to higher end bait caster reel, I like the Quantum Smoke PT low profile.

http://bit.ly/1Q6N01G

An affordable lower end bait caster would be something like the Bass Pro Shops MegaCast Low-Profile Bait cast Reel.

http://bit.ly/1Q6N9Cn

Most of the difference between higher end or better made baitcasting reels may turn out to be castability. Some people have tried lower end baitcasters thinking they couldn't get the skill down and try a friend's higher end model and it turns out to be night and day in terms of their acquisition of performing the cast and feathering the reel spool so as not to backlash. Take a little more time assessing your options for baitcasters than you might for spinning reels. If possible, try them out first.

Most spinning reels today are made left hand retrieve. You crank the handle with your left hand while holding the rod with your right. The majority also make it easy to switch the reel handle to the other side if the angler prefers. This is not so with casting reels. Most casting reels are made right hand retrieve. Most anglers are right handed so this creates a situation where they cast as they normally would with their right hand on the reel, but then must switch hands as the lure hits the water to begin retrieving. This is one of those things that has never really made sense to me. I prefer consistency here between the two styles. Although they are harder to find, there are left hand retrieve casting reels.

I prefer not to switch hands at one of the most important parts of the angling process where I could miss a fish. Biomechanically speaking, my right hand is my dominant hand and, therefore, the most skilled. I prefer to do the techniques of fishing with my dominant hand on the rod rather than my non-dominant hand which might end up with a less than ideal lure presentation on the other end of the line. That's just my preference. If you prefer the same, be sure to look for the left hand retrieve baitcasting reels as they are harder to find and less standard.

Lines

Any beginner angler can get by with normal, monofilament fishing line, in the right poundage for the rod and reel they are using, and fish species, they are fishing for. Recently we've seen advancements in so-called super lines and hybrids such as a fluorocarbon coated monofilament.

It is worth noting that the line, and specifically any knots you tie, are going to be the weakest link between you and possibly a big fish. So be sure to match all the parts of your gear together for the task at hand.

In general, there are three types of line. There could be more classifications, but we'll stick with three to make this section easy.

Monofilament. This is what your father used. It's the old standby. It is cheap and plentiful and comes in a variety of sizes, strengths, colors, and volumes. It can perform nearly any fishing task. This is all we had for some time. Its cons lie in the fact that it has memory, meaning, it will retain a shape it has been forced into for some time (coiled on a reel spool in the off season). It stretches. You may not want that when trying to jerk bait fish, for instance, or have a high degree of sensitivity. It floats. And its abrasion resistance isn't as good as fluorocarbon.

Sunline, has a good brand of monofilament that doesn't stretch as much, casts and handles well. If you get it in clear or green, in the six to twelve pound range, this makes for a good monofilament fishing outfit.

http://bit.ly/1YtuarO

Fluorocarbon looks a lot like monofilament, but it has higher abrasion resistance (supposedly). Some kinds are less visible in water (supposedly). These two facts make it a good leader material choice. It is more expensive. It doesn't stretch. And it sinks. It might be a small detail, but using fluorocarbon with a floating top water bait, might not make the best combination as fluoro can sink. Fluoro also has less memory, but that also makes it want to come off of spinning reel spools easier.

Berkley's Vanish fluoro in the six to twelve pound range can be an excellent bass fishing application especially when you need to go light or when the fish are line shy. I keep a small spool in my PFD all the time for near invisible leader material.

http://bit.ly/23EtMdn

Co-polymer is a line that has a blend of these materials. Often it is monofilament with a fluorocarbon coating. It has better knotting capability, more abrasion resistance, and less stretch. Essentially, you can get some of the benefits of fluorocarbon, but for a few less bucks.

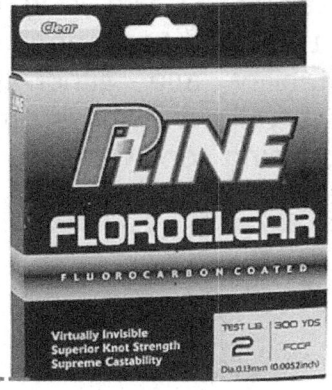

Something like P-Line Copolymer Floroclear represents this class of line well. A spool of this in the six to twelve pound test range in clear is good for most spinning freshwater applications.

http://bit.ly/2bRTojF

Braided lines. There are all kinds of braided lines on the market now. These are the most expensive, but the most durable and long lasting. They allow for a much smaller diameter line for the given strength. It allows for the most sensitivity. The poundage rating is usually much higher than posted on the box. It is more visible in the water and does float. It is hard to cut with nail clippers. You may need a special line cutter like what is in the joint of some pliers to cut braid effectively. It is subject to catching wind. Thicker lines can get water logged and tend to loop up when retrieved on spinning reels. It knots very easily and very tightly. It has a much thinner diameter as the same strengths of mono or fluoro. It casts very far. It is hard to break off. Sometimes you want to break off. If you get a hard snag while boating in moving water, you don't want the line to be so strong you can't quickly get out of that situation. Worse, you don't want to become entangled in it, yourself, at all, or in the water. It is very thin in diameter and can cut into your skin under pressure.

I used two kinds of braid. The most well-known and reliable is probably PowerPro. I use it in the 10-15 pound test range for castability and either the hi-vis yellow or moss green depending on what I am doing.

http://bit.ly/1Sadcgu

The other kind I like is Spiderwire EZ Braid. This has a little more of a slick outer appearance and I think casts slightly better, but seems it may twist more on spinning reels.

http://bit.ly/1T3PL8M

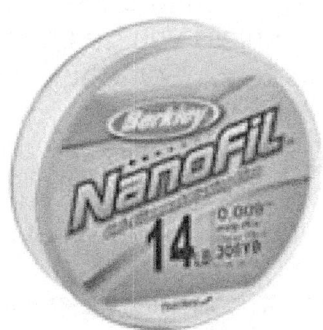

Other lines like Berkley's Nanofil or Sufix could fall into the super line category and may have some characteristics of the others mixed in. Berkley's nanofil is neither braid nor mono or fluoro. It's a compound they call uni-filament made from Dyneema.

http://bit.ly/1TR9fzF

Sufix 832 Advanced is braid, but a mix of fiber types and rounder weaving pattern.

http://bit.ly/1VUUJag

Most of the fishing I do involves some aspect of all of these line types. A normal freshwater bass fishing set up would involve the rod and reel selection above coupled with a monofilament backing on the reel to either an Albright or double Uni knot to braided line as the main line. It's important to have mono backing so as not to use up so much braid, but also to make sure it doesn't slip on your reel spool under tension unless the reel spool comes braid ready. From the main braided line down to a short three to six foot length of about eight pound test fluorocarbon, ultimately to the hook or lure.

Each line can have its own place according to what you're doing and what you'll be fishing for. Casting braided line on baitcaster reels is somewhat tougher unless you go up into the higher poundages and thicker diameters. Some find casting braid easier on baitcasting reels. Experiment with your gear and find what works best for you.

Weights and Sinkers

These are another element you must consider, especially in dark, cloudy waters and or when fishing deep water specifically. There are also specialty sinkers, with rattles, these days to entice the fish even more. Fish are very sensitive to sounds, noise and vibrations in the water so anything you can do to create that allure is great to bear in mind or to avoid if you want a silent presentation.

Sinkers traditionally come in lead, but also come in newer materials like tungsten. Weights and sinkers have many varying shapes and sizes to match your fishing techniques.

For most bass fishing applications, I love using the Water Gremlin Bull Shot Split Bullet Weights. These are very similar to other bullet weights, but they don't slip and have a split so you don't have to cut the line and retie to add or remove one or change sizes.

http://bit.ly/1XvhmAR

Weights and sinkers also come in other shapes such as:

- Round split shot
- Bell sinkers
- Egg shaped sinkers
- Bank sinkers
- Pyramid shaped sinkers
- Coin shaped sinkers
- And specific drop shot weights

More often than not, we tend to stick with bullet, egg, and split shot in freshwater fishing. Sinkers can be tied on midline as you would with a Carolina rig, clamped on with a split weight, pegged in place with a toothpick for a slip sinker, and allowing the sinker to freely slip up and down the line through its middle hole.

Here again, you want to use the right amount of weight for the application you'll be employing, but no more. Wind, current, and depth will all play a role. I find in most river or lake environments, I can get away with anything from weightless baits to $1/16^{th}$ oz to about ¼ oz weights. $1/8^{th}$ is my go to weight selection to fish the bottom of a shallow river, lake, or pond.

Snaps, Snap-swivels, Swivels

These items are what is known as terminal tackle. In addition to being mindful of things like how line shy your fishing target may be, the same holds true for things like snaps. A snap may make it very easy to change baits, and that can be a good thing so you don't have to constantly retie or keep cutting off more of your leader. However, it can also add an element of artificiality to your lure that is already artificial. Fish can be snap shy too. It could mean the difference between nothing and a few more caught fish. If I am some place and only have one rod or so, I may use snaps to help me change baits and pattern the fish. I usually try to use them with moving baits too. Something I'm not going to go low and slow with and sit in front of the fish for a long time to allow them to get a good look at it. Snaps can fail too.

I notice with some of the gold colored snaps on the market, the metal fails rather quickly or falls apart completely. You don't want to lose a good fish just because of some poor metal manufacturing. Additionally, the more metal tackle you have at the end of your line, the more things can get hung up on it. Some snaps have a small wire tag end that protrudes out of the wire gate. Although this adds strength to the snap closure, it is also a great place to hang up grass, weeds, and algae, vegetation types found a lot in Florida waters. Most fish will not bite your lure if you're trailing a big green string of algae behind it. In weedy or grassy areas, you may consider going without this kind of snap.

Snap-swivels are exactly what they say. They can allow the quick change of baits, but also include a barrel swivel. This can be useful in not adding twist to your line. The swivel allows the bait to turn freely 360 degrees. If that swivel were not in place, and you had a bait that tended to turn in circles, eventually, you'll probably end up with a good amount of line twist you'll need to remove. Retrieving or trolling spoons that spin will add twist to your line if you don't have a snap swivel or swivel only in place. Some spoons come with their own, but more than likely, you'll need to add one to your line in order to fish the spoon.

Swivels or barrel swivels do not include the snap feature. These are usually placed further up the line and may attach the main line to the swivel and the leader line to the other end of the swivel. The same function applies by allowing it to freely rotate and avoid line twist, but could also be used concurrently for other things like a bobber stop, a place to attach a weight, something for a plastic bead to clack against, or place to add a secondary line. A three way swivel is useful if you have secondary lines tied to the main line.

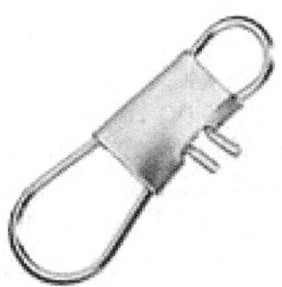

A simple interlocking snap with wire gate.

http://bit.ly/1S6AVvI

An interlocking snap combined with a barrel swivel.

http://bit.ly/1N8qon7

The barrel swivel only option.

http://bit.ly/1RTY6Nl

There's always a time and a place for using terminal tackle or not. More times than not, I'm trying to go without it. I usually have a freshwater bass fishing set up with one of the rods and reels selected from above, with 10 or 12 pound mono backing, tied in a double uni knot to 10 or 15 pound braid for the main line, tied in a double uni knot to an eight pound fluorocarbon leader, tied directly to the hook or lure usually with an improved clinch knot. The more metal and points sticking out, the more likely you are to drag in vegetation in Florida.

Go Here to View a Video on How to Remove Line Twist While Fishing

https://youtu.be/wRpHSaHWUPw

Hooks

There are all kinds of hooks and sizes and little standardization in sizes. The numbers remain the same, but the actual sizes from one manufacturer may not match the actual size of another.

Additionally, whole numbered sized hooks get smaller the greater the number. A #32 hook is the smallest. A 20/0 hook is the biggest. A #4 hook is bigger than a #32. But, a 4/0 hook is smaller than a 20/0. They run on either side of zero. There is no zero sized hook.

There are different thicknesses or gauges of the wire that make up the hook. Usually referred to as light wire or heavy wire.

The hook designs are made with the type of fishing and the target species in mind. There are live bait hooks, J-hooks, barbed hooks, unbarbed hooks, octopus, wide gap, extra wide gap, skip gap, circle, double, and treble. And more.

If you are using treble hooks, try removing some of the hooks so the damage to the fish is less. You can cut off one of the hooks or some anglers take the treble off and replace it with a single hook. Also try using circle hooks if you are using live bait. Just remember to not "set the hook" as much as you would with other hooks. When you get a bite just lift the rod tip to tighten the line up and start reeling, the hook will set itself in the corner of the fish's mouth, usually.

Hook sizes typically recommended around a #4 live-bait hook, sharpened and turned up slightly (say around 10%), this is done to ensure that the fish stayed hooked and gives you a fighting chance to reel it in and land it successfully. A weedless, #5 hook can also serve you well in these conditions. Largemouth bass can be caught at any depth, using a variety of baits, throughout most the year. Sharp hooks are key though. Even if the rest of your tackle is sub-par, make sure your hooks are quality and sharp!

One of the things many fishermen neglect is hook care. Have you ever lost a big fish that was on and wondered why? Maybe, your hook wasn't sharp.

If you fish brush piles, gravel beds, rock piles, log jams, bridge pilings, timber and boat docks you need to check your hooks for sharpness. A sharpening tool should be a regular part of your tackle box or can easily be put in a pocket of your PFD. I have mine there and pull it out regularly. If you're on your way to fish and don't have a sharpener go to a drug store and get a diamond-dust nail file at a drug store. It's important to check your hooks sharpness every time you get snagged.

Here is the way I test my hooks for sharpness:

Grab the shank of the hook in one hand and gently put the point on your thumbnail, don't apply any force or pressure whatsoever. Now, try and move the hook across your thumbnail, if the point digs in then the hook is sharp.

I also use this method for my knives to test their sharpness. Just drag your thumbnail across the blade at 90 degrees or a little less and it should shave off some of your nail if sharp. If it glides over your nail, you have a rounded or dulled edge.

Sharp hooks can make your fishing trip a success or failure. The big one doesn't have to get away when you have a sharp hook.

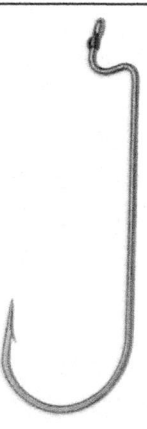

The VMC WM Worm hook is an excellent option for Texas rigging soft plastics on light tackle.

http://bit.ly/1qRRC7c

VMC hooks have a couple of unique features. The eyelet of the hook is covered with a resin to prevent line from slipping through or off. This is a small thing, but if I could have back every moment my knot got hung up on the opening of the hook eye, I'd have been a lot more efficient fisherman. Just a small thing makes a significant difference over time.

The other feature I like is the slightly offset hook point which can translate into better hook ups rather than the point and the shank being in the same plane. You see this a lot with circle hooks in saltwater tackle, but VMC has brought it to bass fishing.

Be sure to keep a heavy wire hook tied on at all times to go to in case you need to throw directly into heavy cover. A light wire hook is great for more finesse fishing in more open areas, but may not hold up if you've got a fish on and several pounds of water logged weeds along with it. A heavy wire hook along with your heavier power rod will guarantee you'll be able to get that fish out of there and into the boat.

Lure Types and Techniques

Fishing Artificial Baits

Spinning tackle and artificial baits and lures are increasing in popularity and the most popular form of fishing worldwide. As far as bass fishing is concerned, it is one of the easiest ways to attract fish, even for novices, and beginner anglers of all ages and fishing styles and skill-levels. Rotation, color and movement, staying as true as you can to the natural diet and target prey of the bass will optimize your chances. The shape and thickness o spinning blades on lures affects the action and mobility of the lure. How it responds and acts in and under water.

Artificial lures can be utilized alone or in combination with live or natural baits. The size and type of lure will depend on the species, location, and style of fishing you prefer.

For bass fishing in particular, a couple of suggestions are to bear in mind that enticing the predators from below, takes skill, practice and patience. Having a handy pair of polarized sunglasses are a MUST! Keep on moving the bait around and play with the presentation through your list of techniques below. It is an art, acquired skill that gets better over time. When casting the bait out, try not to spook the fish, remembering that they are sensitive to sound, noise, movement, and vibrations. Being adaptable, switching baits, different color, and different retrieves until you find the pattern that the fish like and are on at that time.

Most of the time, fishing freshwater in Florida is going to be shallow and weedy. More often than not, you'll be leaning toward more weedless rigs. But, there are times where treble hook baits come in handy too and we'll list many of them and cover that below.

Hard Baits

Crankbaits

Plugs, surface lures, useful at all fishing levels, and at all speeds make these lures versatile, agile and an all-time favorite of many a bass angler. Matching the lure to the conditions you face, the circumstances, body of water, and specific species you are fishing for.

The word crankbait mostly refers to lures, which are usually made from a variety of materials, including hard plastic or wood. With an added feature of a diving lip on the front (simulating effectively the movements of natural prey, wobbling, diving, and swimming actions), entices the bass to strike. The rule of thumb, normally is that the larger the lip, the deeper it can dive. The angle and shape of the lip will matter too. You can go from a wake bait, which swims immediately subsurface to deep diving cranks that can go 25-30 feet down.

Enhancements like rattles are also good for certain conditions. Some crankbaits float, others slowly sink, and others suspend. I find suspending or slow floating crankbaits to be more of what I prefer many times. If I pause the bait, I want it to stay in front of a potentially following fish, not immediately float or sink out of the strike zone.

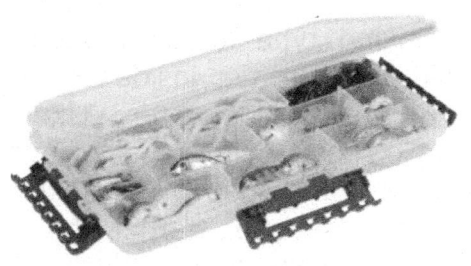

You need a place to store your tackle and lures. The Plano waterproof storage boxes are the best.

http://bit.ly/2bHyN2V

The Koppers Livetarget crawfish crankbait is an excellent mid-level diver with realistic crawfish pattern painted on. I love this bait for river bass action.

http://bit.ly/1SMALcS

The Strike King KVD Square Bill is a great shallow water crankbait good for getting a lot of deflection of rocks and structure with the square bill. Comes with that proven bait fish color pattern. I particularly like these for fishing shallow areas just off from banks.

http://bit.ly/1TRadMj

Lipless Crankbait

This is mostly referring to sinking type lures, made from plastic or metal, sometimes with many rattles inside for noise, , vibrations, and causing disturbances underwater. Like the Rat-L-Trap I described earlier. These baits usually have a shad profile design to them and it is the shape of the body or the flattened head that gives it its action rather than an additional added plastic lip. These baits almost always sink rather quickly. But, you can run them at almost any depth in the water column.

Lipless cranks come in handy in the grass and weed lines in Florida to get a reaction out of bass hiding in there waiting to ambush. You can make a long cast out, let the bait sink into the grass and rip it out and follow with a stop and go retrieve. They may hit the bait as soon as it comes free of the grass. The body profile makes it easy to pull through grass and the heavier power rod allows you to use the backbone to tear the trebles through the grass.

I like to have two styles of lipless crankbaits in my tackle box. One in a bait fish pattern like the Strike King Red Eye Shad. You can't go wrong with this bait. It can be extremely productive.

http://bit.ly/1SafnAw

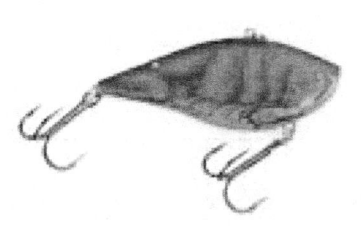

And I also like to have a craw pattern available. Both of these types of baits let you fish anywhere in the water column and switch from a bait fish to a crawfish depending on what the fish are biting that day. The versatility of these baits allows for multiple retrieves, styles, and speeds. The Lucky Craft lipless crawfish crankbait is a favorite. I also like Xcalibur's Real Craw lipless crankbait with the matte finish. Any of these baits from bluish to light brown to darker reds seem to produce well.

http://bit.ly/1oXzg3e

Hard Swimbaits

I absolutely love to fish hard swimbaits. These come in many designs and are usually made of hard plastic with a jointed body. The joints are often metal hinges of different kinds, but could also be made of a strong fabric like Dyneema. These baits typically do not have any diving bill. They are slow sinkers and will have a tendency to slightly rise when retrieved. Many times they also include a couple of large rattles. The jointed body makes for a great realistic swimming action. These baits can be retrieved on a variety of techniques and also do well trolled.

The Cabela's RealImage HDS hard swimbait combines an extremely realistic finish along with very life like swimming action.

http://bit.ly/2locAeV

The SPRO BBZ-1 Shad is a perfect example of this type of bait although I do usually prefer 2 treble hooks on baits like this.

http://bit.ly/1Q6PSvu

Jerk Baits

A seasoned favorite amongst bass anglers for suspended and colder water bass. These baits are longer minnow-shaped profiles, available in lots of different sizes and colors. With a slight twitch and stop type of retrieve, a stop and go, or even as a more slow and steady retrieve underwater, these baits can get finicky or cold bass to bite. This is often the default lure of choice in Winter and early Spring conditions. Another option is to use suspending jerk baits that typically dive deeper, jerking it, almost teasing and tempting the bass to come up and bite at it.

The Lucky Craft Pointer style of hard jerkbait is ideal. You can get it in a slightly smaller 78, or slightly larger 100 model.

http://bit.ly/1S6CRVc

Jigs

Some have described these trusted tackle as "lead head and hook with dressing." Their added features could take the shape of rubber or plastic skirts or soft plastic baits for bodies instead of skirts. Or even tied up with hair or combination of plastic and hair. Most bass experts combine them with a crawfish, or other plastic bait as a "trailer". Even strips of scented and colored pork skin can be added creating what is called a "jig and pig."

Chances are, if you're friends with a lot of fishermen, one of them will make his own jigs. In that case, you may prefer to use his hand made ones and have confidence in them. On the commercial side, jigs come in many styles and shapes with different functions. A swim jig will have a flatter head for planing in the water. A bottom jig may have a football shaped head for added movement when pulled over rocky bottoms. A flipping jig may have more of a bullet shaped head. The hook sizes, lengths, and skirt styles can vary also.

Strike King makes an excellent swim jig with nice shad patterns on the skirts. I like the little bit of red paint on the head and usually trim the fiber weed guard to even with the top of the hook point.

http://bit.ly/1NocfwU

I like the Chompers football head jig. The skirt is tough, the paint stays on the head, and I like the slight curve to the hook shank putting the point of the hook in more of a stand up position when fished on the bottom.

http://bit.ly/1N8rUFF

Punisher makes an excellent hair jig. I prefer this in brown or black. This is another great winter time bait for fishing low and slow.

http://bit.ly/1N8sxit

Hair jigs are tough and don't get torn up like soft plastics do almost every cast. You can keep casting and catching without having to take the time to re-rig or fix a soft plastic you'd fish the same way. Lastly, if used as a crawfish imitation, the wire weed guards look a lot like antennae which I prefer over a fiber weed guard sometimes.

Poppers

Poppers are top water lures that carry long-range punch. The retrieve with these kinds of lures are jerky or move in relatively one spot for a duration of time. They are called poppers because they are designed with a concave mouth or head opening that cups the water and pushes it forward upon each twitch of the retrieve. This creates a popping and disturbance of the water on the surface. They can be quite effective or on days with the right conditions that are early or late and flat calm waters. These baits can be in the shape of fish, frogs, fish, mice, cicadas, or other prey.

A top water strike is one of the most exciting things in fishing. It's often flat calm and near dead silent interrupted by an explosion of water and a big fish inhaling the bait from the surface. Sometimes the fish hit it so hard, their whole body leaves the water.

It's important not to react instantly and try to set the hook right away. With top water fishing, you want to see the strike, wait just a second to be sure the fish has it fully in its mouth, then set the hook. Often fish will hit this bait while you pause it between twitches.

The Skitter pop is an excellent top water popper with a bait fish design. It also includes a dressed rear treble hook.

http://bit.ly/1SzE4n5

The Rebel Crick Hopper is a small popper that can be good for all kinds of pan fish including bass. It looks very much like a grasshopper and is vigorously attacked in most freshwater locations.

http://bit.ly/1Q6RoxQ

Spinner baits

Spinner baits are artificial baits that are specifically designed for the purpose of tantalizing the fish. It is very similar to a jig, but with a blade that runs above the hook attached to a wire arm. It spins and can imitate a school of baitfish. It is meant to provoke, make a strike calling on the fish's natural instinct to feed and or defend. It optimizes your chances of securing strikes if you couple it with a trailer hook. Baits may have a single blade or many blades. They can vary in shape and function as well as color. Rotation, color, skirts, fluttering action all work together to simulate movement and prey on the move.

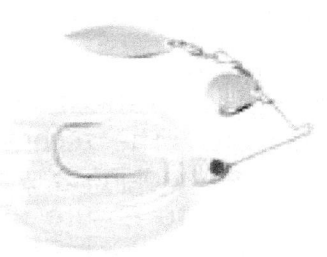

Having a spinner bait with some red in it, simulates blood or wounded prey to our underwater predator, triggering yet again their natural instincts and feeding response, increasing your odds of getting a bite.

http://bit.ly/1oXDDeH

Inline Spinner

An inline spinner is very descriptive of its design. Instead of the hook and spinner being separated by a length of bent wire, the wire is a straight shaft and the hook, usually a treble hook, is at the bottom of the shaft. Along the shaft is some kind of body to the bait. And the spinner blade is attached to the shaft with a clevis which allows it to fully spin when retrieved through water. This is an excellent panfish bait of all kinds. Even trout find it irresistible.

There are a variety of sizes and colors of inline spinners made by Mepp's. I prefer one about 1/8 oz, with a silver or gold blade and dressed hook.

http://bit.ly/1S6GRVF

Soft Plastics

Plastic Worms

There is a vast array of worms available on the market. For avid bass anglers they are a necessity. The technique to master is hooking them properly. When hooking a worm for bass fishing, it is of utmost importance to ensure that you thread it properly. Get a lot of the body onto the hook, and on straight. Otherwise, it may spin and mess up your presentation in the water. When we think of the soft plastic fishing worm, most of us probably think of the original Creme worm or a curly tail plastic worm. Those baits still exist and still work just fine. Today, we often think of baits like the Yamamoto senko or a Zoom Trick Worm.

Yamamoto Senko

http://bit.ly/1SajKM4

Zoom Trick Worm

http://bit.ly/1SajSex

Grubs

Grubs are a very common soft plastic bait. They usually have a rounded curly tail and come in all sizes. They can be used the same as plastic worms, but probably perform best when you swim them on the retrieve letting the tail wiggle the whole way back stimulating bites. Grubs can be extremely versatile. They can be used alone, fished weedless, on jigs, on worm hooks, used as a trailer on spinner baits and skirted jigs, or suspend it below a float.

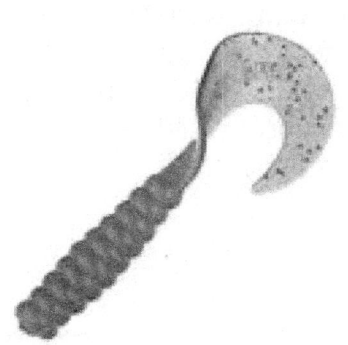

Berkley Power Grubs with Powerbait scent are an extremely effective soft plastic bait. Many times, I tie on a small pumpkinseed power grub with a 1/8 oz. jig head and troll it to my first fishing location just to see what's biting that day. I would often pick up one or two fish immediately.

http://bit.ly/1SajYCY

I believe the Powerbait scent in these grubs adds tremendously to their effectiveness. Under the right circumstances, you could go a whole day using this bait and never change. That is particularly true for river bass.

Crawfish

Crawfish are an excellent bass bait. A three or four inch natural looking crawfish is deadly in a river environment. It is easy to bury an offset hook Texas rigged in a crawfish body with moving claws and legs. Even better, many jig heads with wire or fiber weed guards only adds to the profile looking like antennae or some other extremity.

My favorite soft plastic crawfish is the Zoom Speed Craw. I've had the most luck with this bait in this profile category. It isn't as realistic as other crawfish, but I think it has better swimming action with the claws if that's how you plan to retrieve it. A three inch speed craw in pumpkinseed or green pumpkin is ideal for river bass fishing.

http://bit.ly/1Mu8YRH

Yum Craw Papi in natural crawdad or green pumpkin color. This one still swims with the claws, but not as well as the speed craw, but looks more realistic. Solid tail, hollow body and allows for a great place to insert the point of an offset hook while Texas rigging these baits for total weedlessness. These Yum baits are also scented.
http://bit.ly/23uvQIw

Swimbaits

There are more soft plastic swimbaits than hard swimbaits on the market. The most effective seem to be some kind of paddle tail design, usually in a minnow profile. Of course, there have always been the old swim shad and sexy shad which are still effective too, but now we have a broader design choice in the market. I like a natural colored, white belly, silver sided, black or dark top minnow swimbait. You can rig them on a regular jig head for best results or a keel weighted hook for more weedlessness.

Swimbait minnows cast out fast and far, allowing to let it fall and dangle, quiver down, with lots of slack, might prove just what the fish ordered.

The Bass Assassin Sea Shad might be my favorite soft plastic swimbait ever. It's one of the most productive baits I've ever used and I really enjoy using them. This is easily one of my top five all-time favorite baits. I feel more confident in the thinner minnow profile rather than thicker bodied shad profiles of other swimbaits. This bait just flat out produces fish. Here too, I have gone full days fishing this one bait and never changed lure types.

http://bit.ly/1S6KFpQ

Soft Jerkbait

These can be used to great effect in the same manner as a regular jerk bait, but can be dropped to the bottom quite successfully as well to tease out our deep-water predator, swimming around for food and feast.

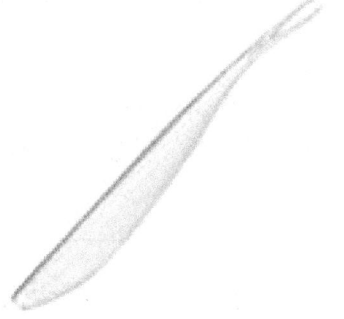

The Zoom Fluke or Super Fluke are excellent fall and spring time soft plastic jerk baits. They seem to do best in white or pearl.

http://bit.ly/1NogtEx

Tubes

Tube jigs and Power tubes that are scented, are other options. The soft, natural chewy substance, tricks the fish, into not wanting to let go and have another chew, thus increasing your odds of landing it safely. These baits can be versatile and resemble swimming bait fish, but more likely crawfish on the bottom. They can be rigged and fished a variety of ways.

Berkley Power Bait tubes are an excellent scented choice for a tube pattern. They work great in pumpkinseed, dark brown, green pumpkin, and black with blue flake.

http://bit.ly/1Muajbd

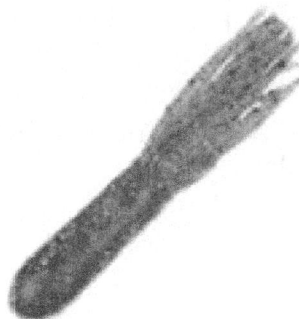

Coffee Tubes are one of the most scented baits you'll find. Something about a strong smell, even of something like coffee, can really trigger bites from fish like bass.

http://bit.ly/22ugBcB

Frogs

Frogs are a favorite food of big bass and a favorite fishing lure of fishermen. Generally, I find two kinds of frogs applicable in most areas in Florida. I prefer the Stanley Ribbit most often. But, there are times where a frog without the kicking legs causing such a water disturbance might be warranted.

These are ideally used in, around, and over top of various weeds in Florida. I particularly like to stop them over holes in the grass to float for a second and wait for a big blow up.

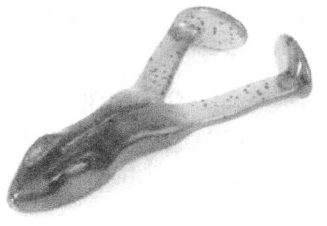

The Stanley Ribbit Frog is a great topwater frog option for fishing around vegetation in Florida.

http://bit.ly/2cttCCu

The SPRO Bronze Eye Frog is another good topwater option around vegetation. It has less disturbance than the kick legs of the Stanley.

http://bit.ly/2cp2y99

Lizards

Lizards are soft plastic baits made by several companies, usually in the five or six inch range. They can be fished on jig heads, Texas rigged, weightless, skimmed on top water, Carolina rigged, and flipped into cover. These baits present more of a creature bait profile with swimming appendages and tails. Green pumpkin, black and blue flake, and purple are all good colors for lizard baits.

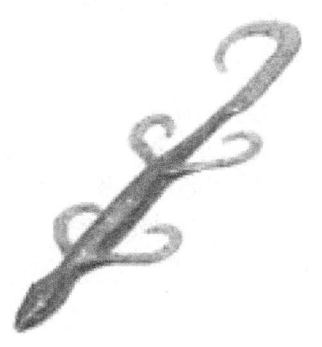

The six inch Zoom Lizard is a great bait to Texas or Carolina rig. You can fish it in and around weeds, on the bottom, or even swim it on top. Lizards tend to work best in green pumpkin, purple, and june bug colors.

http://bit.ly/1SMFmMa

Top Water

Surface, top water and or buzz baits: Acting almost like a spinner bait, but with a curved helicopter like blade that enables it to surface with speed and make a bubbly disturbance. This is a popular choice for many a bass enthusiasts. It attracts the attention of the bass, by creating a disturbance along the surface like a fleeing minnow or other prey, triggering their basic feeding instincts and hunter impulse to strike.

A buzz bait like the Booyah Pond Magic in white has the power to raise a fish or two from the depths.

http://bit.ly/1qHZ5WO

Top water baits with rattles are another all-time favorite, with slack in the line, walking the dog, makes for an enticing presentation for the fish below. However, the conditions must be right for this technique. A windy, choppy water day probably won't be good for a top water presentation.

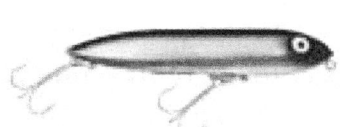

There's nothing more well known for being able to present the walk the dog action than Heddon's Zara Spook.

http://bit.ly/1qoYuc5

Chatterbait

A chatterbait is relatively new to the fishing scene as well. You can think of this lure as a combination of the wobble and disturbance of a crankbait, but the flashy blade of a spinnerbait. The metal blade is shiny, but positioned up front vertically through a connection with a snap to the line. The effect is a rotational wobble in the water similar to the scrounger head's plastic cup or bill. This bait has the silicone skirt of a jig or spinnerbait, but many fishermen also add a soft plastic trailer. I prefer a paddle tail soft plastic swimbait trailer. This can act as a great search bait to locate fish. You can show them a little more flash in the water if visibility is lacking. It can also be retrieved with other techniques such as trolling.

The Z Man Chatterbait in green pumpkin and black with a silver blade is my choice. You can choose a number of trailers from the two soft plastic legs that come with it, to a crawfish, to a swimbait. I often opt for the swimbait trailer.

http://bit.ly/1qRfw3p

Spoons

For spoons, there are two broad categories, namely trolling and casting spoons. Weedless lures mostly have hooks with nylon or metal weed-guards that prevent snagging and are good for use in Florida where there may be heavy vegetation. How to tell which one to use, most bass anglers look for shape, weight and speed. The best way to find your way around in any tackle shop or box, is to practice and get to know the behavior and or success in different conditions. Trying to get to know the optimum retrieval and success rates, maybe even logging it in a personal journal as you undertake your fishing journey.

Spoons act/move in a fishlike manner in the water, trolled behind boats they are typically very effective and can also be casted and retrieved.

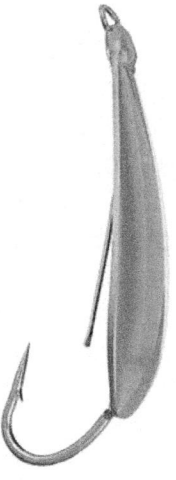

One of my favorite spoons is a Johnson weedless silver spoon. This type of spoon has a little more erratic action in the water rather than just the spinning action of most casting spoons. The Martins are big fans of these spoons at their marina on Lake Okeechobee.

http://bit.ly/2aj68wM

Lure Scents

Sometimes a scented bait makes all the difference in the world. I keep a couple of these in my PFD storage pockets at the ready all the time. I particularly like them on soft plastics. The wand has scented attractant that sticks on the bait longer than a liquid. I like these in crawfish and minnow scents.

http://bit.ly/1V1rdAE

The Bio Edge Minnow Scent Wand.

http://bit.ly/1oXLA3N

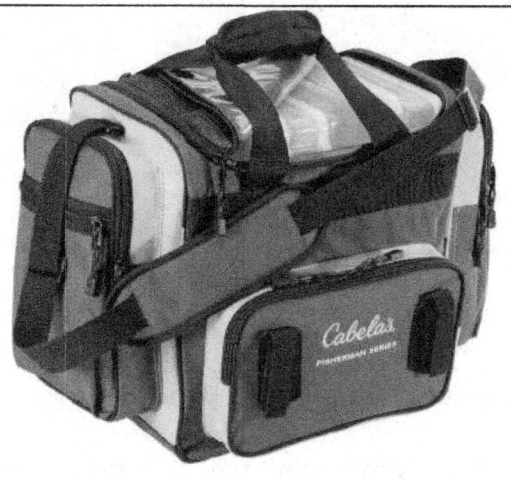

A large tackle bag can be handy for carrying and storage of large numbers of tackle boxes.

http://bit.ly/2bhPAJ3

Go Here to View a Video of Freshwater Lures to Keep in Your Freshwater Arsenal

https://youtu.be/P-XyTeD3RKY

Technique Specific Rods and Staging of Rods

The true secret lies in what some call the one-two punch, teasing and enticing with a teaser lure and then following it up with a plastic worm, for example, on a second rod, for optimizing strikes and tipping the scales in your favor. Now we are getting into the mastery portion of the skills involved in fishing. In chess, a good player will think 3, 4, 5 moves ahead. You can do the same when you start to master your skills fishing. The whole purpose of having multiple rods on a boat is not simply just to have them, but to have technique or lure specific rods rigged and ready to go at a moment's notice. So you quietly pull up to your usual fishing spots where you know fish like to hold. You can start with a cast to it with a spinner bait. If no hits, follow it up immediately with a crankbait. If not hits still, follow it up with a swimbait. And finally a worm or crawfish soft plastic. If you're reasonably certain fish are there, and you haven't scared them off, these types of successive presentations can help you pattern the fish for the day. The pattern being the lure size, type, color, and retrieve. It may take some persistence to determine this too. It may take as many as 5, 10, or 20 casts, maybe with the same lure before the fish strikes. If you're reasonably certain the fish are still there, don't give up.

Some days you'll notice that it is the green pumpkin grub that's the ticket. Some days you'll notice that it's the 6" purple lizard they prefer. Some days, in the morning, they prefer the pumpkinseed tube, but that bite dies down and in the afternoon and evening, they start hitting natural colored swimbaits.

You can do a similar technique as above with your rod staging, but with the same lure and rod. Let's say you have on a 4" minnow soft plastic swimbait. You can cast it out and retrieve it quickly burning it back close to the surface. If no hits, you can try again, but this time with a slower, but middle of the water column steady retrieve. If no hits, you can try slow rolling it back periodically bumping the bottom with it. If still nothing, you can try retrieving it with pauses or twitches. You can yo-yo it up and down jigging it vertically and horizontally in the water column. Lastly, you could cast it out and just dead stick it on the bottom. All different presentations you can try with the same bait.

In fact, from an organization standpoint, if you're not moving too quickly with the wind or current, it might be good to try some or all of these techniques with the same rod and lure before moving onto your other rods and lures. That way, you can really narrow down what the fish are after that particular time and day not only regarding the particular bait, but how they want it presented.

Styles And Specialty Bass Fishing Techniques

Skipping

This technique might remind you a lot of throwing rocks onto the surface of the water to see it skip.

Spinning rods and reel combo is best used for this technique, perfect for fishing and reaching bass where they swim and hide under piers, docks and pontoons. Also useful for getting under and into underbrush and growth. Remember their comfort zone. On sunny days, bass look for shade, food and shelter and often rest here in shady areas, under cover of structure. To employ, simply boat up to a dock or other structure quietly, make a side arm cast at a low angle to the water with something like a slim profile soft plastic so it skips a couple of times to get up under the structure. Let the bait fall weightless. Chances are you'll get a hit right then. If not, you can employ a few twitches, jerks, or some other type of retrieve and try again.

Ripping

Some call this popping and dropping. A medium power, fast action rod or better will likely be what is needed here. It might actually trick our bass friend into thinking there is a wounded prey around. Let the worm drop and settle to the bottom, remaining there for a period of time. Reel some slack out of the line, picking up the worm with a long, sharp upsweep of the rod tip. Let her rip! Let it drop down again to the bottom, under tension while slowly lowering the rod tip. Keep on imitating live prey like this, moving, swimming, and bobbing about and your predator will strike it with a vengeance.

Drifting

Trailing behind the boat, covering the bottom, worms, crawfish, and creature soft plastic baits crawl and move, simulating prey in its purest form. Raise and lower it occasionally, looking natural and alluring to any bass in the vicinity hunting for a tasty morsel. This is a great technique on most fishing trips. I will often tie on a large Texas rigged worm as weedless as possible with no weight or only 1/16 and let it drift behind the boat while I move with the current or wind and actively cast to targets out front. It will periodically grab onto structure or grass on the bottom and then pop off suddenly going back to crawling its way along the bottom. It's a form of more passive fishing. But, the fish will eat it up. I often use a larger bait so as to have a chance at a larger fish while I may be making more finesse presentations actively up front. Some days, you don't have to cast or retrieve much at all. Just put in and float all day drifting tubes or worms or craws and reel bass in one after another.

Trolling

Another technique that can be brutal (for the fish) is trolling. At first I didn't like trolling because I'd always been on charter boats as a kid trolling for stripers in the bay. There's little activity on your part as the customer, you just reel them in like wet newspapers when the bait gets bit. You usually think of this technique while striper or walleye fishing or something, but it's a good Florida bass technique too. You can get slow speeds and perfect the right pace to entice fish to action. You can instantly change speed and direction making some lures on opposite sides of your rigging slow down or speed up triggering more bites. You can troll any bait you want from a boat. Sometimes even idling speed or a trolling motor on the lowest setting may be too fast for some species in a power boat though. You can control the depth of crankbaits better by how fast you go. If you can rig up your boat so that the trolling rods are in front of you, you won't have to continually look back to check on them. This makes the act of trolling much more active and enjoyable. Then, when the action heats up and you get double or triple bites at the same time, it's really a heart pounding adventure.

Drop-Shotting For Picky, Overfished Bass

There is a fairly new technique when it comes to bass fishing but it works great especially when bass are under a lot of pressure, it's called drop shotting. When you see other fishermen using worms and fishing the edges of creek channels, try this and fish the bottom of the channels instead of the edges. It's also good around boat docks and bridges and in shallow water when the bass are bedding.

When fishing the bottom of a channel try a small worm hook with a 3/16 ounce sinker or whatever weight you need to get down and stay there. If you have one already a bell sinker works great, but there are specific drop shot weights now.

Here is what you need to rig a drop shot:

A small octopus worm hook and a 1/8 to 1/2 ounce bell sinker or special drop shot sinker. Tie the hook on your line using a palomar knot and leave enough line after the knot for the depth you want the sinker below it. You're trying to get the lure the right length up the line to be in front of the fish while you can feel the sinker on the bottom. Tie the bell weight at the bottom of the line. It's that easy. Don't drag the bait or hop it, shake it, jiggle it in place. This action gives the lure an erratic tail wiggling action that can entice bass to bite. If your lake has a lot of fishing pressure from being fished so hard or the fish are just picky try this technique and see the results.

Walking the Dog

This is an angling technique that usually requires some time to master, but beginners should not shy away from trying it, for it is quite effective with bass. Casting over a relatively long distance, allow the bait to sit for a brief period of time, take up the slack, and with your rod tip pointed at the water, 90 degrees to the direction of your line, give it a jerk and immediately give the line a little bit of slack, then immediately move it backward and reel in any slack, then jerk again, and repeat all the way back. More or less a darting from side-to-side is made by the lure. You are in effect simulating the prey's elusive movements, enticing the hunter to follow, stalk, and hit. Be sure to add in a few pauses on the retrieve. Many times, the bass will hit while the bait is stationary. The action draws them in to inspect, then they hit it when they get the chance on the pause. This might be your ace up your sleeve for hooking up fish on a good top water day.

Bobber Rigs and Slip Sinkers

Slip-bobbers, rigged with a 1/16 ounce jig, live bait like minnow, night-crawler or leech at its tip and, of course, all on a sharpened hook can be extremely effective for all sorts of panfish. This is a great beginner technique and for kids. But, could also be referred to as a float and fly rig if rigged with a small hair jig.

Jiggling, lightly shaking, presenting this close to any emerging weeds or brush, underwater logs, trees, stumps, or cover, may likely prove successful.

Floating jig heads, with slip-sinker rig, with two to three foot leader have proven to be useful too, especially when kept close to the bottom, watching not to get snagged in the process. Weedless hooks can help you retrieve live bait and or that hooked fish, through very thick undercover.

Free Lining

Fishing in shallow waters may yield many a bass angler quite the haul. Casting a plain J hook with live bait and feed the line to the bait, allowing it to swim while slightly struggling on the hook will attract some certain attention. You can do this with no float, no weight, and either bail open or closed.

Experts would recommend if you are in the weeds or heavy slop, cover, and jungles underwater, to go heavier is the key. 20 lb. line the minimum and heavy power, fast action, sturdy baitcasting rod and reel combos to provide you with leverage to reel in your fish. A large struggling bluegill or shiner on the end of a line could yield you a monster size largemouth bass.

Flipping and Pitching

Flipping and pitching are two similar techniques often confused or used interchangeably. Both are usually performed with bait casting reels and heavier powered rods with faster actions in or around structure and cover.

Flipping is a short distance "cast" to a nearby object that may hold fish. The line, just above the reel is pulled away from the rod brining the lure up to the rod tip. The angler proceeds to swing the lure outward toward the object and releases the line back to the rod and reel allowing the lure to drop in on the object. This is usually performed with a jig type bait with a trailer, but could also be used with a worm. Anything that is a dead stick type bait presentation or it may include a few shakes and wiggles if the bait isn't hit immediately. A rapid succession of short flips can be placed in a short amount of time along a structured area that may hold fish. In this technique, the reel is never engaged.

Pitching is slightly different. It can be used with other baits for more moving and retrieving presentations. Often it is used to pitch a heavy weighted lure (like a jig) up high to punch down through grass mats. But, that isn't the only option. In this technique, the angler swings the lure back up into his non-rod hand. He lets go of the lure while downwardly sweeping his rod tip to "pitch" the lure out to a desired target while thumbing the reel spool. Think of it as sort of an underhand cast. The reel may be set to near free spool with this technique and all the control is done by the angler's thumb on the line. Upon contact, he can let the bait sit or begin his desired retrieve. Some reel models today have controls built in for pitching allowing the angler to press down on the release lever, pitch the bait, keeping the lever depressed while also thumbing the spool. As soon as he lets off the lever, the reel engages closed again. He doesn't need to engage a turn of the reel in order to lock the reel. Both of these techniques can be a quitter or softer way to get your bait in the water rather than a long and high cast where the lure creates a large splash upon entry. These types of settings and this technique can also be a way to make a quick succession of short casts to potentially awaiting fish. More casts and more bait time in the water equals greater chances of hooking up.

Punching Grass

This technique comes in handy in the grass mats in Florida. You'll want to rig up a creature bait or crawfish on a heavy wire offset extra wide gap hook with up to an ounce and a half of weight on a slip sinker on the line. You can pitch it up real high to get a lot of momentum coming down to punch down through the canopy of grass that is covering the water's surface.

Underneath is an entire ecosystem of small bait fish, larvae, insects, and large bass are in there to eat. There are natural channels that open up due to wind and current and various creatures moving through. If you punch down through and a big bass is nearby, it's a good chance for an instant hook up.

If not, give it a few jigs or twitches up and down. You may even pull it back up to the canopy of grass and twitch there. If no strikes, pull the bait out and pitch to the next likely spot.

Again, go with heavy gear here and don't underestimate how heavy a large bass and soaking wet vegetation can be.

Night and Winter Fishing

Dropping the lure or bait right in front of the fish while not having them expend a lot of energy is the key for these times and conditions. Water tends to be cooler and all your approaches, strategies, and techniques need to slow down a notch. Bass also tend to school, during these times. Knowing this fact can help you in acquiring your target better and increasing your odds of getting a hit under these unusual or specialty conditions. They'll be looking for the areas that hold the most heat longest from the sun of the day. There are also spring fed rivers in areas of Florida from ground water that stay the same temperature up to about 75 degrees year round. Obviously, this helps the bass stay warm and active. You'll see other species migrating up river to take advantage of the same like manatees.

Again, understanding what bass actually eat, where and when, will help you with choosing and presenting the most effective, appropriate and tempting bait (whether live or artificial). Drawing on the natural diet of the fish, can assist you in improving your baits and lures appearance, strategy, tactics, and eventual success. Bass, as a predator will be looking for certain shapes, colors and familiar movement. Plastic worms and crawfish are popular choices, but are usually sized down in winter. Another good lure option in these times is the hair jig. Either a dark brown or black hair on a small 1/8 ounce or less jig head. You can fish this bait the same as you would a small tube, worm, or crawfish, only slower during the colder months.

Catch and Release Practices

Some people, but not many still eat bass they catch. The catch and release method was first introduced in the 1950s. It was designed to reduce the rising costs of restocking hatchery-raised fish and was normally used for fish not meant for consumption. This technique is widely used in Florida bass fishing, and may be required by law in some areas. Be sure to check the FWC regulations, and adhere to them, if you plan to keep some of your catch. There will be daily and bag limits. There may also be size limits. These will change over time. Be sure to be up to date on the latest regulations for your area.

Do all you can to understand and adhere to licensing, permits, closed season stipulations, minimum size and catch limits. These and other measures are there to protect and to minimize the risk of over-fishing and species becoming extinct. You can find out more by checking the FWC page for freshwater fishing regulations.
http://myfwc.com/fishing/freshwater/regulations/

Catch and release fishing all the time, by itself, is not a good thing. If you come upon a fisheries management situation where you are asked or allowed to harvest certain species, sizes, or numbers, then by all means, take advantage and maybe feed your family that night too. In general, it can be good over time to remove a few smaller fish from the breeding population to better manage a fishery. You don't want to remove the monsters in a breeding class from a fishery.

Doing your part to protect nature and conserve it for future generations is mandatory and regulated. Holding the fish in the water as much as possible, gently unhooking, reviving them, minimizing the trauma and damage to the fish, especially the jaw, is crucial. Support the fish and let it go with the current, swimming away and left to live another day, for many battles more to come.

There was a reservoir I used to fish where white perch would overpopulate and they asked anglers to harvest them without limit. I periodically took advantage and made some small perch fillets, even fish tacos that were great. I'd even save one small little perch for the cat. Cooked pan fried in butter with salt and pepper then chopped it up like cat food. He loved it.

If the environment presents itself to where culling is needed for control and you can take advantage of the natural resources, and you're well within the legal limits, there's nothing wrong with partaking once in a while.

Fishing Ethics and Etiquette

The way you are perceived and accepted by fellow anglers may not be high on your list of priorities when learning how to fish. However, there are some common courtesy points that all fishermen should abide by to make the experience as pleasant as possible for everyone.

While the rules of politeness may not always be accented in our society as much as it once was, we should have respect for our fellow sportsmen just as they should have the same respect for you.

This also extends beyond treating others with respect, it also entails respecting the resources on which you are fishing. The water, the banks, the woods, and all of outdoors should be treated with common courtesy so it is not damaged for future generations or current property owners. To leave no mark where you have passed in your fishing adventure is showing the ultimate respect.

Here are a few common suggestions of courtesy you should follow when fishing:

1. Wait your turn at a boat ramp. Don't jump in front of others with larger boats to launch. There may be no established right of way at the ramp. Be sure to follow the rules on all signage at the ramp in which you are launching. Generally, I like the elevator principle. People must get out first in order for you to get in. Outside of that, courtesy goes a long way. If you're confused at all, just communicate with the other sportsmen around you to "direct traffic."

2. A section of water belongs to the first person fishing it. It is inconsiderate to crowd an angler who was there first.

3. Obey who has the right of way. Always be on the lookout in your surroundings. Don't assume that they see you. Don't encroach on other stopped or drifting power boats while they are fishing.

4. A slow moving or stationary angler has the right to remain where he/she is. If you are moving, avoid the water they are fishing and quietly move around the angler in position in the water.

5. If an angler is resting the water, or allowing the water to calm down after some form of disturbance, let them be. Generally, after a fish has been caught, the act of the fight scares the rest of the fish and makes them hesitant to bite again, so they rest the water until it is fishable again. They might be planning their next move too. When an angler is resting the water, it is his or her water. Don't jump in without permission.

6. A person working upstream generally has the right of way over someone fishing downstream.

7. Always yield to an angler with a fish on the line.

8. Do not enter the water directly in front of someone already in the water.

9. Do not litter. If you brought it in, take it out. Better yet, always try to leave the water or area you are fishing with more than you came in with. Leave the area cleaner than you found it.

10. Try not to make tracks whenever possible.

11. Wave or wave back to other boaters on the water. It is a friendly thing to do and shows that we are all happy to be out there. It also acknowledges that you see them and they see you.

12. Obey all state and local fishing laws and rules.

13. Never attempt to land someone's fish for them if they have not asked you to help. You do not want the responsibility of losing some guy's lifetime fish.

14. Do not dictate what kind of lure to use unless asked. It is downright amazing what fish will hit on. Let your buddies pattern the fish themselves. If you have good luck and a fellow angler isn't, you might say, "This green pumpkin grub really seems to be working, I have an extra if you would like to try it."

15. Respect others' property rights. That means fences and gates. Close all gates behind you. No trespassing means NO trespassing. You can find out who owns the property and ask permission. Many folks will happily say yes. And you can offer to go above and beyond by cleaning up trash or mowing some of the property another time, etc. However, no really means NO. Sometimes, the landowner may even own a particular stretch of river bed bottom. This is rare, but it is a real thing.

16. Just in case you end up in a situation where some ignorant person violates any of the suggestions above, explain as politely as possible their error. It sometimes works. Maybe no one ever told them about angling etiquette or boating rules or laws.

17. If the person decides his or her fishing is more important than yours, do not stoop to their level. Move on. You probably won't catch anything with them there, and the stress of having to be around such people isn't worth it.

While fishing, your most likely confrontations will be with jet skiers. Jet skiers are out to have fun (rightly so) and rarely have been exposed to the same kind of etiquette that we anglers have. Nor have they been educated on the rules of the water. To us, it can often appear as though they think they own the place. That's ok. You can still use the principles above to navigate your way through these encounters.

Anticipate some of these and don't let anyone ruin your day on the water. Just going with it is better than killing yourself inside or, worse, a violent confrontation. We're all just here to do what we love and it just so happens there is not very much water (even less access points), and a lot of people. If you routinely run into these problems, just consider looking up a different spot. There are many apps and online maps where you can plan your put in, take out, and fishing spots where you hopefully won't be bothered by these confrontations. Better yet, see if you know of someone who has property that might offer a good fishing location or launch site and get permission. Always ask, every time!

People fish to relieve stress, not create it. When you have someone trying to intrude on your peacefulness, it's best just to walk away rather than exacerbate it. Remember that a little common sense goes a very long way when it comes to basic etiquette.

How to Plan and Budget Your Florida Fishing Trip

Planning Your Fishing Vacation

As with any vacation, fishing vacations can cost a considerable amount of money. Planning your next vacation six months or even a year in advance will allow you to save money and give you enough time to purchase equipment, figure out who will be going with you, and find ways to save even more.

During the planning phase, you should spend time gathering brochures, visiting websites, and narrowing down your choices as to where you want to go and the type of water you want to fish.

If you are planning your trip with a group of other fishermen, comparing locations, taking a vote, and coming to a decision as quickly as possible will allow you to save money and make the entire trip less stressful. If planning with a group, you should determine the following:

- Favorite places to fish
- Inexpensive places to fish
- Number of people going on the trip
- When everyone is available to go on the trip
- Equipment everyone already has
- Equipment that will need to be bought (if any)
- Accommodations while on vacation

- Group budget for food, gas, and other necessities

By talking as a group and allowing everyone to give their input, not only will the trip be less stressful, you may also be able to save money. Why buy equipment that people already have? By pooling your resources, most of the equipment costs should be covered.

Creating a fishing vacation budget where everyone contributes money, you will be able to buy bait, gas, food, and other items along the way. While individual members of the group should be allowed to buy any extras they want, the group as a whole should not go over their budget.

Once you have determined where you will be fishing on your vacation, it is time to make reservations, ask about group discounts, and take stock of any additional equipment that will be needed. Creating payment phases will help everyone be able to pay a little at a time so the trip will not end up becoming too much to pay for. If a deposit is required for a cabin or a hotel room, set a date when everyone is to pay their part of the cost.

Keeping detailed notes and updating the group if anything changes or when the date of the trip is drawing near is a good way to stay connected to the group and make sure that everything is ready when the fishing trip date finally arrives.

While you cannot plan for everything, you can plan for most things, especially when going on a group fishing trip.

If you and your group are on a budget, you should look into the following options, which will save you money:

- Local fishing trips to non-tourist hot spots

- Off-season fishing trips
- Half day trips
- Campgrounds instead of hotels
- Group discounts
- Planning a fishing trip within another trip
- Using brochure coupons
- Benefits of price shopping online
- Renting a boat instead of bringing one
- Timeshares
- Reusing equipment or sharing a buddy's

These options may save you a lot of money because they are creative and innovative ways to take a fishing vacation. These ideas will work for large groups, small groups, individuals, and families.

Local Fishing Trips

If you are on a budget, but you want to get a few days of fishing in while on vacation, you can choose to stay local. With so many lakes, rivers, streams, creeks, and ocean access, you have many choices that you can drive to and not have to spend extra money extravagant hotels or cabins.

Research local lakes in your area to see if there are any that interest you. For most people, a day's worth of fishing is enough for them. But if you want to stay for a few days, you may be able to find a lower cost hotel. Keep in mind that you will be fishing most of the day, so staying at the best hotels is not necessary.

Off Season Fishing Trips

Another way to save money on fishing vacations is to look into off-season trip options. Off-season fishing vacations means fishing in waters that are not as populated by fishermen. Those who have rental properties, boat rental companies, and hotels will reduce their prices at this time because they want to attract people who are interested in saving some money on their vacation.

Off-season is different for certain regions and breeds of fish, but typically, the off-season starts at the end of the summer and continues until the beginning of winter. It will pick back up again after the New Year and into the early spring. As a rule, many people begin taking their vacations after Memorial Day, which is the last weekend in May. This is the start of the busy season.

In order to save money, you can choose to rent a cabin or a boat during the off-season. While this time of year may affect the fish population, overall, you will be able to get in a few good days of fishing at a much lower cost.

The best way to take advantage of off-season fishing vacations is to do your research. Find out when prices will begin to drop, where the best fishing is, and how much you can spend.

You may or may not have to make reservations during the off-season, but you should call ahead just to make sure. While you will save money, making reservations is recommended because someone else may have the same idea you have about an off-season vacation. Just remember that winter in south Florida is IN-season. That's when it is very busy from all the snowbirds coming down. That's not true in more northern parts of the state and the panhandle.

When planning an off-season fishing vacation, you should:

- Call cabin rentals, boat rentals, and other hotels to find out when prices are the lowest

- Research past weather patterns to determine when the weather will be clear

- Decide how long you want to stay

- See if you have the appropriate clothing and fishing equipment for fishing in the off-season

If you enjoy being around fewer people, colder weather, and catching different types of fish, then you will want to plan an off-season fishing vacation.

You will be able to watch migration patterns, get a new perspective of the landscape, and adapt to the fishing conditions. Off-season fishing vacations are not for everyone so be sure about what you want when planning your vacation.

Half Day Trips

If you are on a budget, but still want to go fishing, consider taking a half day trip instead of paying for a longer one. These trips will take you only a few miles from home, but you will still be able to get a day's worth of fishing in.

When planning a half day trip, you can plan in advance or you can plan within a few days. If you have fishing equipment, the ability to take time off from work, and gas and food money for the day, then there is little else to stop you from having a great day of fishing.

Half day trips are usually taken by individuals or pairs of fishermen. This is because people cannot always take the same amount of time off from work or from other obligations.

When planning your fishing half day trip, you should:

- Have all of your equipment ready to go the night before

- Get directions beforehand so you know where you are going

- Leave early so you can get a the most time n

- Use GPS equipment to find fish faster and plot resting points and other places of interest along the way

- Try not to feel rushed even though you only have one half day

Half day trips are a great way to unwind, forget about stress, and save money. For those who enjoy fishing during a particular time of year, plan your half day trip so it falls during this time.

Most people get to enjoy the half day trip and take advantage of it whenever they can. Even four hours on the water can seem like a long time to a lot of people.

Campgrounds Instead of Hotels

One way to save a lot of money on a fishing vacation is to stay in a campground instead of a hotel. Not only are campgrounds less expensive, you may also be able to find one that is close to the water. This will make getting ready to fish the next morning much easier.

While you will have to bring extra equipment for camping, you will still save money on a hotel room and eating at restaurants and diners along the way. Equipment you will have to bring includes:

- Cook stove
- Food
- Tent or RV
- Blankets
- Fishing equipment
- Pots/pans
- Utensils
- Paper supplies

Even though you may have to sacrifice comfort in order to save money, campgrounds can be a lot of fun for you and your family and friends. For those who plan on fishing most of the day, staying in a campground is not that big a deal. I took my RV to the fish camp at Lake Rousseau in west central Florida in May and stayed all week for $250. Some hotel rooms could rival that for one night. And the lake was right there. I'd just get off the water and walk right back to camp. There was no time wasted getting to and from the fishing location. https://lakerousseaurvpark.com/camping/

If you are planning a group fishing vacation, you should call the campground in advance and make a reservation. This is especially true during the warmer months in north Florida and the winter months in south Florida. Being able to have a place to stay after traveling is a relief.

Group Discounts

When traveling with larger groups (ten or more), ask for group discounts at campgrounds, hotels, boat rental companies, and cabin rentals. You will be surprised by how much you can save.

Many places offer group discounts, but they don't advertise them. Asking can never hurt, so you should always ask for a discount when traveling with a group.

Types of group discounts include:

- Park admissions

- Fishing licenses

- Hotels

- Hotel restaurants

- Campgrounds

- Public attractions

- Certain fishing equipment

With the money you save, you will be able to spend in other ways. A nice dinner at the end of the trip, upgraded hotel rooms, and other luxuries may become available.

A Fishing Trip Within Another Trip

Trying to sneak in some fishing during another trip is a way to save money by combining two trips in one. If you want to travel with your family and you will be staying near a lake or a river, you can incorporate fishing into the vacation activities. This is also a good way to expose children and others to fishing.

When trying to combine trips, you will have to speak with others who will be on the trip to see if fishing is an activity they will want to participate in or that you can go and do on your own. Many people are excited to try something new or participate in an activity they already enjoy.

When planning two trips, you should:

- Find out as much as you can about the area you will be traveling to. This will give you an idea about the types of fishing in which you can participate.

- Book boat rentals in advance so you will be able during a specific time.

- If staying in the area for a few days, see how much time you will have for fishing and schedule it in advance with family and friends.

- Bring the equipment necessary to fish if possible. Don't spend time buying new equipment unless you absolutely have to.

- Enjoy all facets of your vacation even if you don't get to spend as much of if fishing.

It is important to coordinate activities when planning two trips. While you want to have enough time to fish, you don't want to miss out on other activities. Having a plan in advance will help you make the most of your time.

Many people fish while they are on vacation. This is sometimes the only time they have. Whether it is on a boat or just fishing from the shore, being able to enjoy a hobby while on vacation is a way to reduce stress and relax.

Planning a trip within a trip will help you save money. You will not have to spend money on extra hotel nights or take more time off from work. This is a great way to accomplish many things while on vacation.

Using Brochure Coupons

As you gather brochures and other marketing materials from fishing vacation parks, lakes, and ocean vacation rentals, you may find coupons that are worth taking advantage of. Saving money on lodging, boat rentals, and other items is a great way to afford a fishing vacation. When considering redeeming coupons, you should:

- Ask any questions you have about the terms.

- Find out when you can use them in order to get the full discount.

- Find out if there are any other specials available.

- Ask about accommodations, rentals, and other items that are discounted to make sure they are what you are looking for.

Coupons are usually available for use at any time during an establishment's busy season. While you do not have to arrange your fishing vacation around these times, you should consider them as a way to save money. But if you wait until the off-season, you may save even more money.

Visiting or contacting tourist bureaus is another way to receive coupons to local places in the area. If you will be vacationing for a few days, you will be able to save money on food, activities, tourist attractions, and much more.

Benefits of Price Shopping Online

Another way to find valuable coupons and save money is by researching places to stay, boat rentals, and other activities online. Most businesses have websites. In order to bring in more customers, these businesses offer special deals that are available online only. You can find the following deals online:

- Hotel stay
- Boat rental
- Cabin rental
- Tourist attractions
- Bait and tackle
- Campgrounds

While browsing online, you will also be able to compare prices, amenities, and location in order to choose the right accommodations for your vacation. If you need to rent a boat while on your trip, you should also research boat rental companies in order to find the best deals.

The internet is a great way to begin planning your next fishing trip. Web sites are filled with pictures, contact information, and articles about fishing. You will be able to save money by comparing places, taking advantage of specials and deals, and seeing prices up front.

Renting a Boat

Even though most fishermen would like to own a boat of their own, boats can be very expensive and difficult to store when not using it. If you want to buy a boat in order to take more fishing vacations, you may save money by renting instead.

Finding deals online and in print will help you pay for boat rental while you are on vacation. There are many types of boats you can rent by the day or the week that will allow you to have a great time fishing.

When you rent a boat, you will not have to worry about towing a boat, cleaning it after use, or making sure that it returns home in one piece. By renting a boat, you will also be able to try different types of fishing by being able to travel to different bodies of water.

Even if you live near a body of water, you don't have to buy a boat until you are financially ready.

When renting a boat, you should:

- Be aware of extra charges for insurance, deposit, and other charges.

- Find out if it is less expensive to rent by the day or the week.

- Make sure all safety equipment is on the boat.

- Find out when you need to bring the boat back.

Renting a fishing boat for a few days can be a great experience and one you should consider when planning your vacation.

Timeshares

If you are interested in owning a timeshare by a lake or the ocean, sign up for a free seminar. The company will pay for travel and hotel costs while you are visiting. Not only will you learn about timeshares, you will also be able to fish during your free time.

Since most timeshare presentations are over the weekend, you will be able to find the time to fish.

Even if you don't buy into a timeshare, you will be able to enjoy a small vacation.

When going to a timeshare seminar:

- Ask questions if you have them.

- Find out everything you can about timeshares.

- Be honest and tell the salesperson if you are truly interested or not in a timeshare.

- Find out in advance the types of fishing they have and bring your equipment.

- Most timeshare companies want you to take advantage of everything an area has to offer, so make sure you do.

Timeshare seminars can be a good way to visit a new area to see how the fishing is. These trips will save you money and you may end up liking the area to come back to repeatedly.

With the proper planning, you can save money on your next fishing vacation. Since there are many expenses you will have to pay during your lifetime, being able to save money on vacations will allow you to spend a little extra on travel expenses including lodging and food.

Making a priorities list when planning your fishing vacation will help you decide what is the most important. You should list should rate in order from least to greatest:

- Accommodations
- Length of vacation
- Other activities
- Destination

Spending the money in places you want to will allow you to have a much better vacation.

Florida Bass Fishing Top Spots

Tourists and out of state bass fishermen are very much welcome here with the amenities and lodgings available for them. Boats and equipment are for rent, which provide convenience for travelers.

Since Florida has more than 7,500 lakes available, anglers sometimes face a tough decision about where to fish. It is really very important to consider and narrow down the places you'd like to go. To recap, the following list of top bass fishing areas with bass fishing rentals aims to help anglers find a quality place to catch either good numbers of bass or to catch a trophy bass.

1. Lake George

Lake George is one of the many natural lakes on the St. Johns River. It has extensive vegetation that provides excellent habitat for bass. Wade fishing in eelgrass with plastic worms fished in the weeds and other top water artificial lures are productive. Fishing with live shiners is an excellent method for catching trophy bass during the spring spawning season. Visit Bass World Lodge for accomodations.
http://www.bassworldlodge.net/

2. Farm13/Stick Marsh Reservoir

Anglers in this river can locate bass throughout the reservoir among a variety of habitats, including woody stump fields, submerged canals, and hydrilla. Summer 2004 hurricanes drastically reduced levels of hydrilla throughout the reservoir, which can affect where bass are located. Anglers should keep this in mind when trying to pattern fish. The parking and boat ramp are in the northeast corner of the lake. Plastic worms, spinnerbaits, crankbaits, soft jerk baits, and topwater propeller baits are effective. Wild golden shiners are the top choice for anglers looking to catch a trophy fish. Visit Stick Marsh Fishing Guide https://stickmarshfishingguide.com/. Also under the name Fellsmere Grade Recreation Area on Google Maps.

3. Lake Tohopekaliga

Most anglers here who target trophy bass use live golden shiners during early spring. Shiners are fished near native vegetation or topped-out hydrilla. Plastic baits (worms, crawfish and lizards) flipped along grass edges, hydrilla, and bulrush will also catch quality-sized bass. Spinnerbaits, soft jerkbaits, and chugging baits can also be very productive at times. This lake has some of the best history and stats for numbers and size of bass ever. It also has man-made fish attractors. You can go to this link and access a map with their locations so you can find them yourself. http://myfwc.com/fishing/freshwater/sites-forecast/ne/lake-tohopekaliga/. There is also the number to call the Kissimmee Fisheries office to get more information on the fish camps in the area 407-846-5191.

4. Lake Kissimmee

Lake Kissimmee is the largest of five main water bodies on the famous Kissimmee River in central Florida. Lake Kissimmee is nationally renowned for producing high quality fishing. Tournament anglers on Lake Kissimmee are posting winning weights of 18 to 20 pounds of bass. Results of an angler survey indicated that bass anglers had an excellent catch rate of 0.54 fish/hour during spring 2004. Book a trip on the "Freelancer" at https://www.orlandobass.com/.

5. Rodman Reservoir

Rodman Reservoir, east of Gainesville and south of Palatka, covers 9,500 acres of prime largemouth bass habitat. Since its creation in 1968, Rodman Reservoir has been known for trophy largemouth bass. https://rodmanreservoirfishing.com/

6. Lake Tarpon

Anglers in this lake are most successful in flipping or pitching plastic worms along canal and bulrush edges. Offshore bass fishing is productive for anglers who fish around ledges, humps, coontail, and eelgrass beds. Popular lures offshore include shad-imitating baits, crankbaits, jerkbaits, and topwater baits. Fishing with wild shiners and live shad is also effective. The FWC reports this lake to have great numbers and size of the bass population and low fishing pressure making this easily a top 10 lake in the state for bass fishing and it's just a short drive from Tampa.
https://www.laketarponbassfishing.com/

7. Lake Walk-In-Water

The lake is located south of Orlando and east of Lake Wales, and it is just south of S.R. 60. Lake Walk-in-Water has a national reputation as an outstanding spot to catch largemouth bass. Anglers frequently catch up to 25 bass a day with several ranging from four to eight pounds. The lake also produces many trophy bass exceeding 10 pounds each year.

A 15-24 inch slot limit regulation and a three-bass daily bag limit are in place to help maintain quality bass fishing. Anglers may keep three bass per day, either under or over the protected slot range of which only one bass greater than or equal to 24 inches is allowed.
https://www.hawghunter.net/lake-walk-in-water/

8. Lake Istokpoga

Istokpoga is the fifth largest natural lake in Florida and has an average depth of only six feet. During angler surveys

conducted from October 2003 throughout May 2004, anglers caught 124,993 bass of which almost 55,000 were 2 pounds or heavier and 1,448 bass were over 8 pounds.
http://myfwc.com/fishing/freshwater/sites-forecast/sw/lake-istokpoga/

Contact Henderson's Fish Camp at 863/465-2101, or Cypress Isle RV Park & Marina at 863-465-5241

9. Deer Point Lake

Deer Point Lake is a popular largemouth bass fishing destination in Florida's panhandle area near Panama City. There is a fishing pier on the northwest side of the dam and Tharp's fish camp on the west side of the lake.
https://tharps-camp-cedar.business.site/

10. Suwannee River

The Suwannee River is a pristine, black water stream flowing 213 miles in Florida from the swamp-like region at the Georgia border to salt-marsh tidal creeks at the Gulf of Mexico. This river is known for trophy largemouth bass, but also offers the opportunity to catch a Suwannee bass too. The river can experience low water levels. According to the FWC, nearly all the bass prefer crawfish lures here. The craws are king. Be sure to check the contact numbers on this page for more information about visiting.
http://myfwc.com/fishing/freshwater/sites-forecast/nc/suwannee-and-santa-fe-rivers/

11. The Everglades

The Everglades are south Florida marshlands intersected with over 200 miles of canals. Most anglers report the fish are in the canals rather than in the marsh. Anglers work canal edges with plastic worms, soft jerkbaits, and minnow imitations.

Flipping the vegetation is also a popular technique. Contact Hai Truong for Everglades and Peacock bass fishing http://www.haitruongfishing.com/.

12. Weeki Wachee River

The Weeki Wachee river is a beautiful spring fed river in West Central Florida. The state park gets busy and full on the weekends, but you can launch further downstream at Rogers Park. This is an ideal paddle craft river or small motor boat. You may not find the monster bass in here, but there are plenty of largemouths ready to bite in numbers. Small soft plastics on a moderately fast retrieve can work well here. This is a bass fishing experience not like many others where you'll clearly see your fish strike in the crystal clear blue water of the river. As a bonus, you're likely to encounter manatees and other saltwater species of fish making their way up river. You can view a video of bass fishing this river here. https://youtu.be/v9zpKHxt5Wc

13. Lake Rousseau

Lake Rousseau is a large lake northeast of Crystal River. This is an interesting fishery created by the dam in the Withlacoochee River. Below the dam, you can fish for all the typical saltwater species. Above the dam, there is a deeper section that will hold fish. The entire lake covers over 1300 acres and is situated next to an excellent fish camp and RV park. This lake harbors a healthy population of 10+ pounders that the fish camp regularly keeps track of caught by fishermen. Among the fish, you may see other wildlife like a few gators and more bird species than you can count. The lake is full of weeds and vegetation. It also has clearly defined channels and some shallow water obstructions like sand bars and stumps. This is great for fish, but can make power boating a challenge if you don't know what you're doing.

A paddle craft is perfect for this lake although it is large and puts you close to the gators. The environmental department actually has a chemical drip system upstream to help hinder the growth of some of the invasive weeds. Top water and weedless soft plastics will most likely be necessary here. Fast retrieves due to the clarity of the water and the fish's keen senses will be necessary too. Soft white jerkbaits and large Zoom white worms appear to coax the big fish out of their hiding places. Fish the weedline edges adjacent to channels. Fish topwaters through the surface weeds and pause them over holes in the vegetation. Be sure to skip a few soft plastics under the docks as well too.
https://lakerousseaurvpark.com/camping/

14. Lake Harris

Lake Harris is a 13,000 acre lake near Leesburg, FL. You can access it from Singletary Park. In addition to largemouths, you also have the opportunity to catch the sunshine bass in this lake. Sunshine bass are a hybrid of white and striped bass. They like crankbaits, spinners, spoons, and jigs. You can contact Lake Harris Lodge for accommodations.
http://www.lakeharrislodge.com/

Wherever you decide to go, you can be sure that you can have the time of your life fishing and do so conveniently. You can just rent out a boat and eliminate the need to tow your own a long way if you have one. Other gear is also available as a rental for your convenience and ease. There are also many lodges and inns plus cabins and campgrounds you can rent out for a weekend or more to have the ultimate bass fishing experience in Florida. I encourage you to pick some dates and an interesting location from these pages and start to get what you need ready to hit the water soon for some Florida bass.

About The Author

Chris Lutz is a former kayak fishing guide on the Potomac River and surrounding lakes and a Florida native. He has fished every coast and many freshwater locations in Florida while traveling full time.

He is the owner of S.P.A.R.T.A. Fishing (www.spartafishing.com), kayak fishing company and blog. Chris has been fishing his whole life and specifically kayak fishing since being introduced to the paddle sports in college in 2000. His mission is to help you have more fun, be a more successful fisherman, and spend more quality time with your loved ones.

Made in United States
Orlando, FL
05 May 2024